SECRETS

OF THE

WORLD

CUP

ADVISORS

CHUCK FRANK & PATRICIA CRISAFULLI, EDITORS

MARKETPLACE BOOKS, INC.
Columbia, Maryland

This book, along with other books, is available at discounts that make it realistic to provide them as gifts to your customers, clients, and staff. For more information on these long lasting, cost effective premiums, please call John Boyer at (800) 272-2855 or you may email him at john@traderslibrary.com

ISBN 1-59280-196-X

Printed in the United States of America.

1 2 3 4 5 6 7 8 9 0

CONTENTS

A Word About the World Cup Trading Championships®

In baseball, it's the World Series. In football, it's the Super Bowl. In trading, it's the *World Cup Trading Championships®*. In a recent feature story, National Public Radio referred to **World Cup competition as "The Oscars of Trading."**

The *World Cup Trading Championships®*, with separate divisions for futures, forex and stock traders, have provided the **premier arena for competitive trading since 1984.** Each World Cup event brings together serious traders in real-time, real-money competition with national bragging rights on the line.

Contestants vie on a level playing field for prizes, unique World Cup Bull and Bear trophies, and a possible spot on the advisory team at www.WorldCupAdvisor.com.

The concept is simple: Traders showing the highest percentage increases win the top prizes. Entrants can even elect to compete in a voluntary cash prize pool, featuring 100% payouts. **At the end of the day, the best traders prevail.** Winning performances have run the gamut, from a modest 53% futures division return in 2001 to the historic 11,376% by Larry Williams in turbulent 1987.

The World Cup Trading Championships® are products of Robbins Trading Company and Robbins Securities, Inc.

INTRODUCTION

When you manage a brokerage firm, as I do, you quickly learn your clients' priorities. Prompt, reliable service is No. 1. A reasonable commission structure is No. 2. Access to attractive investment alternatives and ongoing education runs a close third. And, from day one, clients have clamored for my firm, Robbins Trading Company, to identify talented money managers and promising new trading models from which they could study and learn new techniques. In our fascinating and fickle industry, this last priority can be the tallest of all orders to fill.

One summer afternoon in 1983, some of my key employees and I were enjoying a day of sailing on Lake Michigan and found ourselves discussing this very issue. Although our firm had grown quickly and we were already offering a wide range of trading products and services, our clients wanted more alternatives and more methods that would help them become better traders. We were trying to think outside of conventional approaches when someone suggested that we entice private traders and potential managers to compete against one another. From that tiny seed a giant plan evolved. We would create a controlled environment in which top traders would compete head-to-head, utilizing their own funds, in an ultimate trading "gut-check and acid test." This competition would separate the real producers from the pretenders — and crown a champion who would truly be the best of the best. Or, as we dubbed the ultimate victor, a World Cup Champion.

As our mission took shape, we resolved to do it right. Ours would be a real-time, real-money trading competition, one that would attract upper-echelon contestants and identify the best futures traders. If we could develop a format that would accurately identify the top trading talent — amateur or professional — we could offer fund management and model development opportunities to the winners. And, using the input and ideas of the various champions, we could provide our clients with the new trading paradigms, strategies and alternative investment vehicles they had been asking for.

It sounded easy. We would publish the format, promote the event, keep track of the results, hand out trophies and publicize the results. How difficult could it all be?

We soon found out. There were rules and regulations, sponsors and expenses, logos and graphics, spreadsheets and newsletters, lawyers, government agencies, trophy molds, advertisements, account forms, documents and disclaimers. We learned quickly that conducting a big-league event of this nature requires an enormous commitment of resources — but I've never once regretted the decision. For me personally, the *World Cup Trading Championships* have been a constant source of both satisfaction and fascination. Over the years, I've learned many new concepts and valuable lessons from the talented contestants. And now — finally — I get to share these interesting stories, strategies and lessons with a wide audience in this book.

Since the first *World Cup Championship* commenced on February 15, 1984, this glorious experiment in competitive trading has spawned close friendships with world-class traders like the incomparable Larry Williams, Chuck Hughes, John Mills and Robert Bloch, to name a few. I've followed the progress of each year's competition on a daily basis and marveled at the displays of skill, patience, resiliency and — in some cases — reckless abandon.

Looking back over the years, the inaugural competition in '84 hardly resembles the competition as we know it today. There were fewer competitors back then and less hoopla surrounding the event. Today's competition is big business with a large cash prize pool at stake and the making of careers in the balance. The initial event was four and a half months in duration; today's championships extend a full calendar year, with traders testing their mettle through seasonal ups and downs.

I remember being duly impressed when our first winner, Ralph Cassazone, generated a 264% return, and I wondered if that kind of performance could be duplicated year after year. When Ralph came back the next year to post an amazing 1,283% return, I wondered if we would ever see a performance of that caliber again. Then — just two years later — Larry Williams did the unthinkable, recording an astounding 11,376% profit, making us all realize that in futures trading, there simply are *no* boundaries.

I watched with admiration and fascination as Larry's account grew by leaps and bounds in '87. When I noticed that it had crossed the seven-digit threshold at the end of August, I did something I would not normally do.

Until then, I had never seen a client accomplish such a feat. Larry's account had grown by more than 10,000%. And, though the second-place competitor was not even remotely close, Larry was still trading up to 1,000 bonds in a single day. At this point, I went against my own financial interests and called Larry to suggest he throttle back his trading. I told him that it was crazy for him to continue to jeopardize his amazing accomplishment. He was paying me a tremendous amount in commissions every day — and if he just sat on the account until New Year's he would still have a landmark finish and achieve notoriety both for himself and the World Cup.

Larry replied calmly. "Joel," he said, "I can't quit now. I'm up over a million. I have to see how far we can take this thing." I could not argue much after that. He is a trader. And traders trade. It's as simple as that.

Sure enough, over the next several weeks in September Larry doubled his account. He was up over $2 million when the stock market crashed in October 1987. Larry's account came tumbling down with it. Remarkably though, his account dipped below $1 million for only a few days. He made a nice recovery and finished with an astonishing $1.1 million dollars. In this book, Larry discusses the '87 victory for the first time in detail. I think you'll be fascinated to explore the emotional side of that wild ride with him. None of us will ever forget '87. Thanks for the memories, Larry.

Although no one has ever come close to accomplishing what Larry did, I have seen some remarkable traders follow in his footsteps. I don't know if anyone will ever blitz the field like Robert Bloch did in '98 and '99, posting five top-three finishes in division competition. And I think it may be a while before anyone accomplishes what John Holsinger did in 2002, finishing first and second with separate accounts that appreciated 608% and 304% respectively. But — the fun part is — you really *never* know. Out of left field, another unknown trader will post another remarkable finish using his own unique methods, from which we can all study and learn.

Over the past 20-plus years, there have been competitors from all walks of life, trading a wide range of markets in a variety of ways. However, they typically fit into two main categories: Technical traders who analyze historical price data to develop systematic strategies, and fundamental traders who base their trading decisions on the analysis of underlying factors effecting supply and demand. On balance, I have found that the systematic traders have been more consistently successful in World Cup competition, although there have been a handful of exceptions. I have observed that when system trading is practiced properly, it takes much of the emotion out of trading and eliminates traders' two worst enemies: Fear and greed.

System traders *expect* to incur drawdowns (losses experienced by the account over specified periods of time, from equity peaks to equity lows prior to recovery), and they realize that they may occur before profitability is achieved. When using fundamental trading techniques, it is often difficult to pull the trigger after incurring three or four consecutive losses. Following a system, in which drawdowns are anticipated, can help eliminate this hesitancy. System trading boils down to one cardinal rule: **Plan your trade and trade your plan**. The system-trading winners of the *World Cup Championship* have proven that this simple adage can pay big dividends.

Part of the beauty of the *World Cup Championship* structure is that all techniques are welcome and all traders begin on equal footing. Last year's defending champion has no advantage over a first-time entrant.

I'm proud to say that this format, based on our daydream in 1983, has become the gold standard of trading. Competitors can now compete in separate divisions for futures and futures/options, stocks and stock/options and forex trading. Entrants can choose from discounts and premiums offered by many respected sponsors, including industry-leading publishers and providers of trading software and data transmission. The World Cup concept has even been licensed in Japan, where the *Robbins-Taicom Japan World Cup Championship of Futures Trading* has been thriving since 2001.

Around early 2000, however, I realized there was an ingredient missing from the World Cup formula. The talented individuals we had identified needed a platform from which they could share their expertise with a trading community beyond my own brokerage clients. And again, from that small gem of an idea, a large multi-faceted plan emerged.

First up was a web site devoted to the World Cup Champions. With the help of Chuck Frank, an old friend with nearly 20 years of experience as a broker and trader in the 30-year T-bond pit at the Chicago

Board of Trade (CBOT), I launched WorldCupAdvisor.com. The premise of this site is to showcase select trophy winners from the competition, by broadcasting their actual trading activity in real-time. In other words, past World Cup Champions show *what* they do, *how* they do it, and *how* they make fast, decisive moves "live" for all to observe and learn from. We were lucky enough to enlist the support of many of our most experienced traders, including the aforementioned Williams, Bloch, Hughes and Mills. I'm very proud to say that the nucleus we established at the site's inception is still largely intact today. And, along the way, we've added a few fresh faces and expanded the roster to include many "non-competitive status" advisors, such as Austin Passamonte, whose trading expertise has been established outside the World Cup arena.

On September 18, 2000, Larry Williams funded his first WorldCup-Advisor.com "Live Update" account, and we were off to the races. Currently, we feature dozens of "Live Update" accounts, which allow our subscribers to monitor and learn from a variety of trading styles and markets. Our traders are baring it all. You can actually view the full account activity of these champions — their orders entered, open positions, closed positions and commentary — and, thereby, gain insights and expertise by learning from some of the best in the business.

And now, with this book, the exemplary ideas, concepts and methods of this truly world-class collection of traders can be shared with an even wider segment of the trading community. After watching traders from all walks of life compete against each other for so many years, I've noticed certain characteristics and habits that are common to our champions. I feel that any individual investor or active trader can learn some valuable lessons from both the victories and the failures of the World Cup Champs. The missteps they've made along the way are often universal to all traders. But the moves they took to rebound from them and trade their way to victory are so powerful that virtually any investor or trader will benefit from these insights.

Nearly all the World Cup Champs learned their most valuable lessons from their biggest mistakes. Rather than packing it in or becoming devastated by their losses, the champions typically step back, analyze their missteps and use that knowledge to make sure it never happens again. In the first section, John Holsinger and David Cash provide their own unique accounts of the best lessons they learned by losing — and they lost *big* — and how they rebounded and ultimately posted spectacular returns. As a long-time trader, I related to the experiences of Holsinger and Cash — and I'm confident you will, too.

In section two, Kurt Sakaeda, Neil Peplinski and Chuck Hughes outline how and why they developed their systems — and reinforce the importance of having such systems. With the advent of the computer, Internet and fast and simple software programs, monitoring charts and using technical trading techniques is easier and more effective than ever. Section three reveals unique technical approaches used by two of the champion traders. Section four highlights a professional advisor — Austin Passamonte — who reveals his own unique swing trading techniques which are ideal for today's short-term traders. And finally, in the last section, the legendary Larry Williams opens up for the first time to discuss candidly how he achieved his astounding results in the 1987 World Cup competition, and how his trading has evolved over time. Larry's honest and frank input is compelling reading for traders of all experience levels.

As I embark on yet another year of World Cup competition, I remain as fascinated by — and passionate about — the trading markets as ever. They're enormously challenging, yet rewarding on many levels. They're volatile and unpredictable, yet they can be a powerful ally if you have the necessary education and discipline. It is my great hope that this book will provide you with both. I invite you to sit back and read the intriguing perspectives of these notable traders. Each has valuable insights that can help you shape your own trading style.

Joel Robbins,
President, Robbins Trading Company

PART 1

THE LEARNING CURVE

When it comes to trading, the market is often the best teacher, as the trading markets have been known to humble even the most astute players. The learning curve is usually quite steep, and the lessons often painful and typically learned only *after* significant losses are experienced. Regardless of your professional background or educational pedigree, losses *will* occur. If you seriously want to become a truly successful trader, three things are necessary: Accept that losses will happen, acknowledge that you do *not* know it all, and make a strong commitment to learn from your losses so you can guard against making similar mistakes on future trades. In other words, if you put aside much of what you know — or think you know — if you have an open mind and no ego, your chance for sustained trading success becomes infinitely greater.

To illustrate this point more clearly, the book opens with two World Cup Trading Champions — John Holsinger and David Cash — whose early trading experiences mirror those of most traders I've encountered over the years. You will easily relate to what these two have gone through, and you may even have a sense of déjà vu as you recall with agony similar incidents you've experienced. The lessons they learned during their evolution from novice trader to trading champion are lessons we can all benefit from.

In the initial stages of their trading career, Holsinger and Cash both racked up sizeable quick and easy gains, which convinced them that the trading game was much simpler than others claimed — and that they were *really* good at it. Their confidence level was high, and they continued trading without some of the discipline and the hindsight that is essential to successful trading. Then came the staggering losses, in some cases wiping out their entire trading account.

Despite repeated crushing blows to their trading accounts, they came back each and every time, driven by a strong desire to succeed. This required a frank analysis of what they did wrong and forced them to embrace the lessons the market was trying to teach them. Their dedication paid off not only in profits, but also in their distinction as World Cup Champions. Explained in their own words, their first-hand accounts of what it took to get through the learning curve — and what they learned by losing — are truly universal.

First up is John Holsinger, who accomplished an unprecedented "double" in the *2002 World Cup Championship of Futures Trades,* capturing the title with a whopping 608% return, while also nailing down second place with a healthy 304% return in a partnership account with system designer and friend Mike Dietch. Originally an accountant by profession, Holsinger's victory and dedication to the markets led to a new career as a Commodity Trading Advisor and president and principal trader of his own trading firm.

Holsinger recounts the roller-coaster ride that brought him from a trader who dabbled in the markets and lost it all on more than one occasion to his World Cup victory. As he notes: "Indeed, it has been a very interesting and challenging journey with a steep and sometimes painful learning curve. From my fascination with the market to my education in futures trading, I certainly hope my experiences will be informative and helpful to others."

David Cash, the 2001 winner of the *World Cup Championship of Futures Trading®,* opened his first trading account with $20,000 and the firm belief he could turn it into $1,000,000. Six months later, he was completely wiped out. That $20,000 loss, however, was a powerful teacher and, ultimately, helped Cash perfect his overall approach to the market. As he observed, "My initial loss — while costly at the time — produced meaningful lessons for achieving and sustaining profitable trading. I've discovered that, while conviction is very important, it alone is *not* good enough to be successful in futures trading."

Cash's journey on the learning curve is even more impressive, given the fact that in 2001 he went on to join an elite group of traders who have won the World Cup title in their very first attempt. On the surface, Cash's 53% return winning performance may actually seem downright mediocre when compared to the returns of other World Cup winners. But it's important to note that he captured the title during a notoriously difficult and brutal trading year. In fact, he more than doubled the account appreciation of the second-place finisher.

Successful trading is not easy. It requires education, discipline, dedication, and, for most traders, a systematic approach. While the *World Cup Championship* has allowed me to see some spectacular returns, even the best of the best have experienced downturns and devastating losses. What separates champs like Holsinger and Cash from the rest of the pack is their ability to swallow their pride and step back to learn from their mistakes in order to succeed as winning traders. Even in the face of mounting losses, they were able to analyze what they did wrong rather than abandon the process, and make the next round of trades even more successful. It sounds so simple. But it's so easy to overlook when you're down in the trading trenches. For that reason, I'm starting the book with this subject — before moving on to the more technical applications the various "champs" have used to achieve their success.

The first two chapters are wonderful illustrations of why working through the learning curve to develop a disciplined, methodical trading system is so important. You will gain insight into the markets from an insider's perspective, as a participant right on the front lines.

CHAPTER 1

LOSSES, LESSONS, AND LEADING THE PACK IN TRADING

BY JOHN HOLSINGER

By profession, I am a certified public accountant with a small practice of my own. As part of my practice, I was often involved in examining investments, and I quickly gravitated to the stock market. Over time, both my professional and personal interest intensified and I soon became hooked.

When I first began to actively invest, the hot vehicle for stock market speculation was OEX options. Over the next year, I not only plunged into these markets, I purchased various black-box computer systems designed to help trade the OEX more profitably. My overall return for this period was probably a wash, as I experienced both up and down periods — but it was certainly exciting, and motivated me to move on to commodity trading strategies and techniques.

After doing some basic research, the first one I explored was the T.E.D. spread, in which you go long Treasury bills (T-bills) and short Eurodollars, hoping to profit if the yields on the Eurodollars rise. It's a basic "flight to quality" play. The risk was small and the margin low, so I put on a T.E.D. spread with a 10-lot position. Sure enough, the spread worked like a charm. I was quickly up 40% on the month.

Buoyed by my success, I took some riskier steps and tested my skills as an "economist." I decided interest rates were headed lower and I dumped the short Eurodollars half of the spread, but remained long on the 10 T-bill futures.

Sure enough, over the next couple of months rates *did* fall and T-bills went up. I tripled my money and congratulated my "genius." Unfortunately though, I made a critical mistake and learned a painful but valuable lesson in the process: Apparently, I never put a stop in the market. One day, while I was tied up in a business meeting, a news flash crossed the wires that the Fed had raised interest rates. By the time I was able to leave the meeting and get to a phone, my position had imploded. I still made some money, but gave back a huge chunk of my profits.

Despite this costly experience, the "up" periods were enough to fuel my desire to keep trading — and to tackle some new areas. I read up on a wide range of different trading methods and plunged in once again after I discovered the immense potential rewards of day trading S&P futures. I soon discovered the perils as well. The OEX trading I had done previously involved holding a position for at least a couple of days. The prospect of making money without holding an overnight position seemed like a dream come true. I purchased another trading program and began to trade S&P futures with the remainder of my stake. But just as I started trading it, the system suddenly went into a horrific drawdown, knocking me completely out of the commodity business for a while.

> **"Instead, I let this third very costly loss startle me into action. Ultimately, it led me to the most important step in my trading education. I decided to educate myself much more intensely."**

Once I had accumulated more capital, I began to revisit commodity trading. Having determined that my original losses had been born out of greed, and having not yet confronted fear — that *other* emotional demon in trading — I began looking at methodologies that offered a smoother equity curve and an approach that could earn a substantially higher rate of return with more controlled risk. Through my research, I found a seasonal trading program, and decided I liked what I saw: High rates of return. Low drawdowns. Very high accuracy per trade.

I immediately opened an account with $30,000 and had the trading firm place the trades for me. I was riding high for about one year before the system went into a multiyear drawdown, and I lost 45% of my original investment.

With three strikes against me — I was at the crossroads. I could walk away and claim that the trading game was not for me. Instead, I let this third very costly loss startle me into action. Ultimately, it led me to the most important step in my trading education. I decided to educate myself much more intensely. I started buying everything I could on the commodity trading business. After reading dozens of books, I began to see a pattern: Although everyone assumed that there was a perfect order to the market, I had yet to find someone who could put it into simple rules that I could follow to duplicate similar results in my own account. What I was looking for, I later discovered, was a mechanical approach to trading. The appeal was enormous. If you put the rules down on paper, they could be back-tested and verified.

Once again, I was mainly interested in the stock index futures. I talked to developers and researched their systems. I purchased the ones that looked promising and paper traded them. The next big development was the introduction of TradeStation software, which facilitated both implementing systems and back-testing them. I had made a lot of progress up to this point. I was ready to have a go at it again.

As anyone can tell you, it is one thing to casually scan the trade-by-trade reports of a system, but entirely another to put it into action. Even with the assistance of packaged programs and software that would spit the orders out, the human element was still faulty. I would pass on certain trades, which were almost always a huge winner. I'd jump back in determined to follow the computer, take three losing trades and then quit the system. Over the next year, I jumped into and out of six or seven systems, all at exactly the wrong time. (Was this a steep learning curve or what?) I was once again forced into retirement.

Instead of walking away completely, I continued to track the systems I had purchased. Six months went by and I watched the systems churn out returns. I started an Excel spreadsheet and loaded in the last three years of performance statistics, day-by-day, system-by-system. Each system had its own column, summarizing the wins, losses, drawdowns, and most of all the bottom line. Surely, there was some information to decipher here.

> **❝If I could remove myself as an element in the process, I believed I would be successful. I needed to become more disciplined.❞**

It occurred to me to compare my own miserable performance with the numbers that the spreadsheet suggested. There was a huge disparity in the numbers. Then it hit me. There wasn't a problem with the systems (that's not to say there aren't bad systems). The problem was *me!* I was getting in the way. I was making decisions based on instinct. Panic. News reports. Fear. All kinds of emotions. If I could remove myself as an element in the process, I believed I would be successful. I needed to become more disciplined.

Back at the drawing board, I sifted through the information in my spreadsheet and refined my process for selecting systems. I began to sort the tables so that I could see which systems offset the performance of others. By diversifying, I was smoothing the equity curve. I discovered some of the systems shouldn't be traded together as they only added to the misery of a drawdown. Some of the systems were helpful in terms of using varied entry and exit techniques. Very quickly, I was able to arrive at a short list of candidates for trading. The final selection process involved proper capitalization. I had lost a lot of money up to this point — even though my portfolios also had periods of very substantial returns. But at this juncture, I had to make the portfolio fit the amount of money I could commit. Once this step was accomplished, I was ready to go back into trading.

My approach, however, was significantly different this time. Since I was already working with a firm that traded the systems I was using, I gave them authorization to place the trades in my account. I never overrode another signal. Does that mean I was immediately successful? The futures market will test you at every turn. Three days after I opened the account, I was already at the maximum theoretical drawdown. It was a Friday afternoon and there was no way to get out of my trades. I had to wait for the market to reopen on Monday. The end result was that two weeks later I had recovered from the drawdown and was up 30%.

The ultimate lesson I learned from this evolution was that I needed to remove myself from the equation; I needed to become more disciplined. Does that make me any less of a trader? I hardly think so. It's simply moving to a "big picture" approach and away from the "can't see the forest through the tree that's falling on me" one. The results speak for themselves. Over the next three years, my initial $40,000 stake grew to over $1,000,000. Of course, good luck and strong market conditions were also working in my favor. But once I did research on pinpointing the right system for me — and removed my emotional decision making from the process — my results were both consistent and astounding.

THE ROBBINS' WORLD CUP:
TRADING WITH REAL MONEY
IN REAL-TIME

So, how did I go from mild-mannered accountant dabbling in the trading markets (and wiped out on three separate occasions!) to World Cup Trading Champion? It didn't happen overnight. It took a strong dedication to learning everything I could about how the pros did it. I read trading book after trading book and studied various methods and techniques. I also analyzed my own mistakes thoroughly and altered my trading behaviors so I wouldn't repeat them. I familiarized myself with as many methods, tools, systems, and software products as I could — so I was able to select the right combination that suited my own temperament and trading goals. Then — and only then — was I ready to enter the competition.

My strategy upon entering the *Robbins' World Cup Trading Championship* was to day trade S&P futures from my competitive account. While some cautioned that it would be tough to make any money day trading, I felt it gave the best bang for the buck. And, there are specific guidelines I follow that, I believe, help curb the risk.

When I day trade S&Ps, I look for a trend. I am only interested in taking one trade, perhaps two, each day. I pick trades very carefully. Normally, I do not trade early in the day. Instead, I watch the market action for the first couple of hours to determine, according to my criteria, what the trend of the day is. To do that, I watch a bar chart of the S&P 500 futures. I usually watch a longer-term timeframe, anywhere from 30 minutes to an hour. Many traders I know watch much shorter timeframes, such as five minute or even one-minute intervals. For me, that is just too much information, therefore I stick to the longer timelines.

I do not use any indicators, just pure price action and chart patterns. I look at the chart and compare the prices to certain key points — such as the open and the previous day's close. As the day develops, I look at new highs or new lows in the direction of the trend. These relationships can be clues as to where the market is *likely* to go. And, as a day trader, I try to bet where the price is going to be at the end of the day. I want to get in as early as possible, and hang on throughout the day.

In the following three examples, you will see more clearly how I follow the trend on a daily basis, what I look for throughout the day, and how I make decisions on what my daily position should be. These are actual trades taken in my contest account which will help illustrate exactly what I look for and how I make trading decisions.

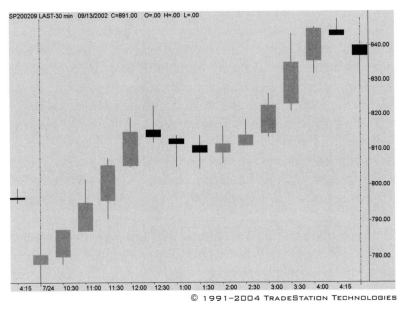

SP200209 LAST-30 min 09/13/2002 C=891.00   O=.00 H=.00 L=.00

© 1991–2004 TRADESTATION TECHNOLOGIES

CHART 1.1   S&P TRADE JULY 24, 2002

This was an outstanding day. I got long at 813 and exited that day at 839 for a profit of $6,500 per contract. This trade was made at a time when the stock market was falling out of bed. Of course, money can also be made by going short, as I did on the very next day.

JULY 24, 2002: The S&P started lower and put in a bottom early in the day. Of course, we don't know that then, but we can watch through the morning. By lunchtime, the S&P has moved above today's open and yesterday's close. It spends the next couple of hours consolidating sideways. Knowing this, I am ready to buy a breakout to the upside and hopefully hang on until the close.

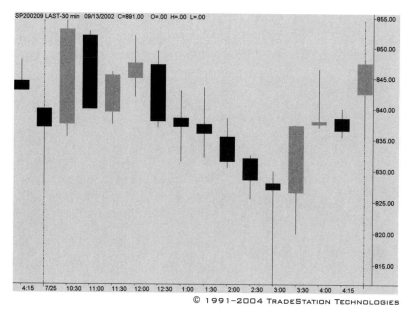

CHART 1.2   S&P TRADE JULY 25, 2002

On this day, I sold at 835 and got out at 821 for a profit of $3,500 per contract. As you can see, the market was really moving over the summer, providing terrific opportunities whether it went up or down. The key was to determine the trend early and then hang on.

JULY 25, 2002: Again, here's an example of early price action that can guide us to trading later in the day. The S&P opened lower and then rallied throughout the morning. Once lunchtime was over though, it had come back below the previous day's close, a powerful sign that it was headed lower. Here I was, looking to sell a break below the support established in the first half of the day.

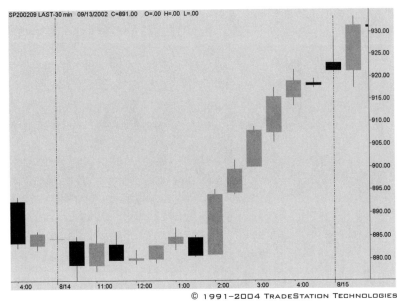

© 1991–2004 TRADESTATION TECHNOLOGIES

CHART 1.3   S&P TRADE AUGUST 14, 2002

This was another great day for my system. I went long at 894 and exited at the end of the day at 912 for a profit of $4,500 per contract. Not all days were as productive as this one, but it showed the power of riding the trend through the whole day.

As these examples show, my objective, once a trade is established, is to stay with a position for as long as possible. This brings up another concept that is equally important: time of day. When do you make your entry once the trend has been identified? There are tradeoffs in this decision. Obviously, the earliest you *can* enter is at the open, and some traders find it rewarding to get in right at the day's open. To do so successfully, you must have made a

AUGUST 14, 2002: On this day, the market was very quiet in the morning. Because it was hovering right around the previous day's close and its open, I was faced with mixed signals. In situations like these, I have to keep an open mind about the markets direction. Again, I watched it consolidate through the lunch hour, and placed an order to go long if the market were to break out. When it finally did, it did so with authority. I actually wasn't expecting this kind of large move, but my system kept me in for the ride.

determination from the previous day's action as to the direction of the market. This can be both hugely rewarding and very risky. On the plus side, you may get in at the earliest possible point on the trend. On the negative side, you may step in front of a freight train headed the wrong way. My advice is: If you want to trade this way, put your stop in and head for the golf course. Watching the market all day will wear you out and tempt you to tinker with your trade.

When day trading, my preference is to enter later in the day, which gives you time for additional analysis, and to observe more closely what happened at the open. The following bars may confirm your decision and you may enter later on, catching a piece of the trend. So what does this mean? Simply put, it means that the earlier price action can give you clues as to where the market may go *by the day's end*. First, I rarely catch the top or bottom of the move. If the market is marching up and making higher highs and/or lower lows, I'll be looking to position myself long. In the reverse situation, I would be looking to position myself short the market. But I have used the first few hours of trading as a *guide* rather than basing my trading on my opinion about the market's direction

The extra insight you get from a slightly delayed entry may not be as exciting as plunging in on the open but I find the confirmation data and ability to use tighter stops to be a huge advantage. Also, I tend to be more mentally alert during the critical period towards the end of the day, if I haven't been in the throes of a trade since the open. In the final analysis though, each trader must choose an entry timing that best suits him or her. Over the years, I tried a number of scenarios. I entered some positions at the open, and at other times I waited until later in the day. But only after trading with real money will you truly know what suits you best. Looking at charts of past trades will not tell you how much stamina you possess. There is no way to duplicate the pressure of being underwater in a trade all day with two hours to go before the close.

Once I decide which side of the market to be on, based on the trend and where to make my entry, the real work begins. Now it's time to consider money management. Or, put another way, how much risk I'm willing to take on a particular trade. As a day trader, you have many choices. How do I make a well-reasoned choice? Let's look at a losing trade as an example of the process I use for determining how much exposure I'm willing to have.

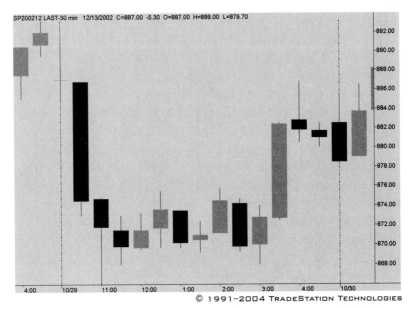

SP200212 LAST-30 min 12/13/2002 C=887.00 -5.30 O=887.00 H=899.00 L=879.70

CHART 1.4   S&P TRADE OCTOBER 29, 2002

It hurts to even look at this trade. With such a beautiful set up to short the market, I went ahead with the trade and ended up taking a loss. This is going to happen in trading. The key is to have a stop loss that keeps you in a trade long enough for it to work out, but preserves your capital when you're wrong. So how do you set your stop loss? This is an area of much debate. Do you use a time stop? Do you look at highs/lows or pivot points? Do you use a fixed dollar amount? Do you use a percentage of your equity?

In my contest trading, I used a fixed money management stop loss. A fixed money management stop loss is a certain amount of money that you are willing to risk on any partic-

OCTOBER 29, 2002: Once again, the market gave us a very clear signal about its intentions in the first few hours of trading. It opened below the previous day's close and moved lower from its open all morning. This was a very clear indication to my system that the market was headed lower. It had made lower lows and lower highs all morning. I sold the market soon after lunch in hopes that the trend would continue lower. This was a trade that was clearly indicated by my system, and I took it.

However, markets can and do change direction and in this case the system had caught a losing trade.

ular trade. For example, you might decide to risk $1,000 per trade, which would be 4 points in the big futures. If you risked $2,000 or twice that much, it would be 8 points in the big S&P futures.

I had made the decision to use a fixed money management stop loss by examining several series of trades to see how much rope I had to give the market before it hangs itself. I personally have never been a fan of using support or resistance points. Although they look good on paper, in real-time they have let me down. This is probably due to the difficulty of specifying criteria for such points. Sure, you can see a place on the chart that never got hit, but how do you define it? If you lack a hard and fast definition, you will end up "seeing" things in real-time that make you jump out of a trade. The same goes for a time stop. Should I get out of a trade after two hours if it's not working? Maybe three hours? I've sat in trades all day and had them come back and make money in the last half hour of the day.

The other disadvantage I find with these type of stops is that you can't build a solid money management program. A more effective approach is to use a percentage of your equity or some fixed dollar amount that you are willing to risk. This makes trading decisions more like business decisions and removes some of the emotional intensity.

What about targets for your profits? I often thought about using a predetermined price target to exit, which offers a lot of mental satisfaction. However, I did not use one in the contest. I think my decision has born itself out. No trading system or methodology is accurate enough to guarantee you 80% winning trades. If it could, the trades would be too small to cover commissions and slippage. You have to hit a home run every now and then to make your money. Everyone wants to hit singles and doubles, but it just doesn't work that way in the S&P futures. You have to be able to swing for the fences.

One thing I will do is use a trailing stop. A trailing stop is a stop level that is changed based on where the market is moving. It can be used to lock in profits as the trade moves in your anticipated direction. Notice that I said as the trade moves in your favor. I won't move my stop unless I have already accumulated some winnings. When this happens, that is when the trade becomes profitable, moving the stop in the direction of the trade can help you avoid taking a loss due to the release of sudden news that could alter the market's temperament. A trailing stop still needs to be far enough away that it won't interfere with the natural fluctuations of price but will still offer you some assurance that should something unexpected occur, your loss will either be smaller than your original one or perhaps you'll even make a small profit.

To reiterate, I only use a trailing stop once the trade is profitable or the market is moving in my direction. I never reduce my stop for any other reason. My analysis has shown that using a trailing stop does not enhance my bottom line or reduce my drawdown. It does take some of the pressure off, however, and since trading is a mental game it is a welcome relief.

Now, let's take a look at one more trade example from the last few weeks of the competition.

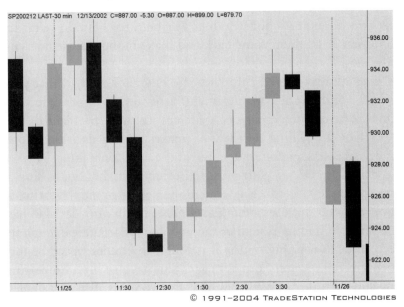

© 1991–2004 TRADESTATION TECHNOLOGIES

CHART 1.5   S&P TRADE NOV. 25, 2002

Now, even though this chart isn't as pretty as the previous ones, I still managed to make about a point and a half on a long trade. I included this trade because in late 2002 the market was consolidating in a tight range. The moves weren't as dramatic as in the summer, but the same rules worked.

November 25, 2002: This was a day when the market moved quite a bit, but had gone nowhere when it was all said and done. The earlier price action of course illustrated a solid down move. I placed my order to go short and was never elected (i.e. the order was not filled). After the window had closed on the chance to go short and my entry was not filled, the market had established a new trend to the upside, as evidenced by the making of higher highs and lows all afternoon. Very late in the day, I placed an order to go long. The market didn't get a chance to run very far at this point, but I still managed to make a decent profit. This illustrates the fact that we let the market action put us into a position. If the market can't continue a trend far enough to fill our order, that is telling us something. In this particular case it told us that the move to the downside had run out of steam.

Succeeding at the Game of Trading: The Seven Basic "Truths"

So why did I persevere even after being wiped out completely on more than one occasion? It's simple: I find trading very exhilarating. It can also be gut-wrenchingly frustrating. But to me, it's very exciting — and very rewarding — once you nail down several key steps. Through my experiences being on both sides of the balance sheet, I've discovered seven very basic "truths" about trading that I now use as my guide posts. Some may sound alarmingly simple. But trust me: You need to take them very seriously if you want to succeed for the long haul, and not experience the same early losses I did.

1. **Determine if you are really ready.** Face this tough question and be totally honest with yourself: Do you have the courage to continue in the face of adversity and loss? If not, then move on, because you will experience periods of loss, frustration, and anxiety as an active trader. However, if you have the constitution for it, then give it a whirl.

2. **Take it seriously and debunk some myths.** Trading is not a get rich quick scheme. Yes, the money can be fantastic, but fantastic returns will only come from hard work. Ignore anyone who claims they can make you a whopping percentage return. I know what you're thinking: Didn't I just admit to making those kinds of returns myself? Yes, I did.

But I didn't promise I could do the same for you! And I only achieved them after I made a harsh, critical assessment of my methods and realized that attaining quick and easy money was only a fantasy.

3. **Understand the nature of the markets: No single decision is the right one.** Trading is not a zero sum game. Yes, there is someone on the opposite of every trade you make, but you don't know his or her reasons. If someone sells me an S&P contract, that person may be hedging a portfolio. Even if the market goes up and I make money being long, the other person still made a rational decision to get out by guarding against potential downside risk. And — if I decide to bail out on a position — it could work to the advantage of someone else with a different strategy.

   Statistics show that 90% of new traders quit after losing money for a host of reasons: They are undercapitalized. They jump in and out of systems at the wrong time or they have wild expectations of profits. I think it's easier to trade if you understand that the markets exist primarily to transfer risk among market participants.

4. **Develop a viable system.** Any good trading strategy must make money. In other words, it's not enough to have a clever idea; you must have an exploitable system. It's not enough for a pattern to appear and repeat itself; it must also make money. And, it needs to make enough money to offset its losses and cover commissions and slippage. Does that mean a system must be highly accurate? I don't think so. I have long ago given up the quest for the proverbial Holy Grail. What a system must do is catch a few great moves. Most of the rest of the time you will be churning around, making a little, giving back a little.

5. **Understand and accept that drawdowns do happen.** This seems to occur after you have been on a terrific winning streak and think you can do no wrong. Or, perhaps, as soon as you start a new system. My strategy has always been to stick with a system as long as possible. Every system is going to exceed its maximum historical drawdown by definition. But a new maximum drawdown does not mean the system has failed. It means it is going through an inevitable cycle. However, only you can decide when the pain is too great. Personally, I hate quitting a system and then watching it come back out of a drawdown. This is also very closely related to

how well you are capitalized. In general, the greater your risk capital, the easier it is to sit through a drawdown.

6. **Understand that systems don't make you money — the markets make you money.** Think about it. You can't design a system that makes money all the time. You need to be patient and wait for those times when the market favors your system.

7. **You must be disciplined.** This is the most important principle. If you learn nothing else from my painful story, it is this one fact. Trading even a marginal system with good discipline is far more likely to produce a positive outcome than haphazardly trading a great system. Trading is mainly a mental exercise. I talk to people all the time who say their system is doing great. When I ask them about the results, however, the reply is usually a string of rationalizations about why they didn't take this or that trade. The cycles weren't right. The stochastic had just rolled over. I only trade on alternate Tuesdays... All of these excuses simply mean you are not committed to the position or the system. And your lack of discipline is sabotaging your trading results. Every legendary trader — and every successful active trader — will tell you this is the key that opens the door to sustained trading success. I learned it myself the hard way. But I can guarantee you it's the most important step you can take on your learning curve.

Looking at my performance over all, it was a mixed bag both competitively and emotionally. For the first couple of months of the contest, I was close behind the leaders, probably up about 100% after three months. It was a little discouraging that I was still behind the pack even with that kind of return. In late April, I moved into the top three. I stayed in third for a while, waiting for some increased volatility to help me out. Finally, in June, the markets were friendlier towards me, and I moved into first place with a return of a little over 200% at that point. Through luck and discipline, I managed to finish there.

I believe this same opportunity awaits anyone who will take a consistently disciplined approach to his or her trading. I see it proven every year, as regular "Joe Traders" go on to win the World Cup. But to do so, you must endure and work through your own learning curve, making mistakes, learning from them and developing the discipline to follow your trading system. From my perspective, the rewards will be well worth the effort.

CHAPTER 2

WHAT LOSING $20,000 TAUGHT ME ABOUT WINNING

BY DAVID P. CASH

I opened my first futures trading account in April 1999 with $20,000; by October, it was gone. Since that loss, I have invested a great deal of time and effort in asking myself why. Why did I lose that money so quickly, when I was convinced I could turn it into $1,000,000? My initial loss of a $20,000 account, while costly at the time, has produced meaningful lessons for achieving and sustaining profitable trading. What I've discovered is that while conviction is important, it is definitely not enough to be a successful trader. In this chapter, I share with you several of those lessons as well as comment on the system development that I have implemented as a trader and in becoming a World Trading Cup Champion.

The ability to build and sustain profits in trading requires a significant commitment of time, effort and capital. As part of that commitment, before you start to trade, you should examine a number of issues, from your mindset to the style of trading you prefer. A careful study of these issues can reduce the time between when you start trading and when you turn profitable. After my shocking $20,000 loss, I did some soul searching and self-analysis.

A TRADING PLAN BEGINS WITH THE TRADER

The following is a list of factors I have found to be critical to sustained trading success, including my World Cup victory.

■ **Ask yourself why you want to trade. What are your expectations?**

When most traders ask themselves why they want to trade, the answer probably seems obvious: to make money. Looking deeper into the question can reveal some insight about a trader's motivation that can separate them from the crowd and possibly foretell their potential to make money. There is both pain and pleasure in trading. Anyone can deal with the pleasant side of the business as they watch their profits grow. It's dealing with the painful side that requires steely determination because the pain of losing money will most certainly test your resolve, as it did mine.

Trading futures is a dramatic business with emotional extremes. Traders must be able to handle the emotional swings in order to survive and thrive. It also doesn't hurt to have something to prove either. Whatever your rationale, take a critical look at yourself and consider what you want out of the business — and what you are prepared to do to get it. If you are half-hearted or feel rather cavalier about the whole thing, then you are better off moving on to something else. If you find within yourself strength and commitment, then you may just have a chance.

■ **Do your research, study, and read. Learn everything you can about profitable traders, especially their perspectives on trading.**

Research and study are fundamental requirements in trading. Learn as much as possible about how winners trade and how they think about their trading. What rules do they follow? What is their perspective? In my personal experience, I talked to my mentors, I read everything they had ever written, and I attended their seminars. From this study and experience, I learned one immutable fact: Trading is about discipline.

The foundation for successful trading is building a plan and having the discipline to follow it. The better organized and structured the plan is in its development and execution, the greater its chance for success. When I began trading, I used a "shotgun" approach, putting my money into as many different markets as possible in the hope that the net result would be more winners than losers. Even though I was equipped with the necessary tools to analyze and trade the markets, I had no plan for using them. I was too anxious to make money. So many traders are thus inclined. They are impatient and undisciplined. They want fast money and are not necessarily concerned with the details of how to obtain it.

Little wonder then, that the lessons the market teaches in these instances tend to be very expensive.

■ **Find your trading style. Know what type of trading — day trading, short-term, or long-term — suits you and your personality.**

As you develop your trading plan, the first consideration should be your trading style: long-term trading, short-term trading, day trading, and so forth. Long-term traders will take a position and hold it for two or three weeks. They seek to capture market trends rather than inter-day or intra-day volatility. Long-term trading was too slow for me, however. (This was the style I mostly used during my first six months.) I grew impatient with the long periods of the trades. At the other extreme, day traders take multiple positions and are in and out of the market several times in a single day. For me, day trading was the "antacid special." I did not care to be glued to a quote screen for five to seven hours a day, watching every little tick of the market.

Short-term trading and the popular swing trading style suited me best, with the right balance of trade frequency and interaction. Short-term traders take a position and hold it for a day or two, up to a week at the most. Short-term trading requires your attention on a daily basis, but also offers some degree of detachment. In other words, you can take a position in the morning and walk away from it for the day. This style of trading provided the perfect balance for me.

Before you begin trading or if you have been trading with only limited success, research different trading styles to find the one that is best suited for you. This compatibility will contribute to the likelihood that you will trade more consistently and successfully.

■ **Choose Your Market.**

Choosing a market to trade is an essential element of your trading plan. There are many practical reasons for selecting a market, including leverage on your money, market liquidity, margins, the degree to which the market trends, and volatility. In addition, traders often take into account the market that their mentors trade. In general, here are a few guidelines for picking a market to trade:

■ **Liquidity:** Pick a market that trades more than 5,000 contracts per day.

- **Volatility:** Make sure the market has good intra-day price action. This feature is more important for short-term and day traders.

- **Trends well:** The degree to which a market trends is an especially important consideration for long-term traders.

As I began trading, I looked at market margins, liquidity, volatility, and trends among different markets. I steered away from currencies because of large overnight gaps, orange juice was too thinly traded, and the S&P margins were too large. When it came down to making a decision, I followed my mentors: Larry Williams and Miles Dunbar both of whom traded 30-year Treasury bonds. I found the bond market to be a good one to trade. It trended well, had good intra-day volatility, was very liquid, and offered a reasonable margin for the leverage.

The characteristics of the market must be balanced in relation to your own temperament, trading style, and account size. Further, there is the point of focusing on a single market. Successful trading requires study and the formulation of a trading decision based upon this study. The more markets you trade, the less time you'll have to devote to each. This is a simple point, but one that cannot be overlooked. The more focused you are and the more time you have to study one market, the greater your chance of being in sync with that market's movements, and thus being correct in your trading decisions.

I do look at a number of different markets and I develop trading systems that work across a spectrum of markets, but I only trade one market at a time. For some people, trading two or three markets at a time is comfortable and right for them. But on the whole, traders would do well to limit their focus to one, perhaps two markets at a time.

INVESTIGATING TRADING "HOTLINES" AND TRADING YOUR OWN SYSTEM

Markets are like nature: One day, they will shower goodness and bring forth fruit, and the next, they'll threaten to crush you and destroy your crop. As in nature, your ability to forecast and contend with such a threat in the markets and manage this risk will play a large role in your odds of survival. This is where a trading system comes in. Each time you enter the market, you should know how and why, what the odds are for success, how long to stay in, how much money to risk, and how to get out. A trading system should, at the minimum, establish these parameters.

That being said, you may not have the time or inclination to build and trade your own system, or you may want to build your own system, but not know how to go about it. What can you do? Another approach is trading hotlines, following the advice of a market analyst or trading advisor. Trading hotlines can be a great service, but they can also be a disaster. Speak with the hotline advisor you are considering. Get to know these advisors and watch their services for a time before committing any money. When you are ready to subscribe to a hotline service and put your money behind the posted trades, keep the following points in mind:

1. **Even the best traders lose money from time-to-time.** As much as you might be compelled to think or hope otherwise, there is no such thing as a perfect trading system or the perfect trader. There is an element of randomness to the markets. Since human beings are trading them, there is an emotional element to the markets that cannot always be predicted. The smartest, best organized, and most disciplined among us will fail to predict correctly every move of the market.

2. **Don't trade with money that you can't afford to lose.** When I send a check to my broker, I do so with the expectation that this is money I will never see again. You should be able to do the same. If you are uncomfortable with this concept, then think twice about your decision. Trading may not be for you or you may not have enough discretionary funds. (This point applies whether trading a hotline or for yourself.)

3. **The minute you decide to commit money to the markets, the hotline will start to lose.** This is one of the "Cash's Laws of Trading," as I call them. It may not always come to pass, but it is a practical consideration. You should expect to take losses when you start out and must ensure that you have plenty of capital to absorb these losses before the next winning streak.

4. **Not all hotlines are created equal.** Choose a hotline that offers as much "behind the scenes" information as possible. Be well informed on the decisions that you make with your money. Look for a service that offers toll-free phone and email access to the hotline advisor.

5. **Just because a hotline makes money doesn't mean it's for you.** Hotlines and advisors who run them have a particular style and approach. Determine whether the style and approach of the hotline and the advisor suit your temperament and trading goals. For example, how often does the hotline trade? How long are the positions held? What kind of positions are they? What kind of commentary comes with the trade? Look for a hotline that has a good track record of making money, and also uses a trading style that you are comfortable with.

6. **Trading discipline, system drawdowns, money management, and account capitalization are all important when trading hotlines.** You must be disciplined, taking every trade that is posted and following the rules of each to the letter. It is important to be adequately capitalized. To do this, you must know the drawdown of the system and the money management rules used to trade it. Discuss the system drawdown with the hotline advisor and ask for money management guidelines for trading the system.

When it comes to trading systems — whether you develop them yourself, buy a system, or trade through a hotline service — keep the above six points in mind. All things being equal in terms of a given system's quality and the research that went into its development, there are two things that will ultimately determine how well it performs in real-time:

■ **How faithful future market behavior is to the historical market trends used to develop the system.**

■ **How disciplined the trader is in following the system's rules.**

While we have no control over the former, we have complete control over the latter.

FOCUSING ON DISCIPLINE

When it comes to historical market trends determining future market behavior, every trader should understand that the past does not necessarily predict future performance. This is part of the risk of trading. Your focus should be on the disciplined application of a system's rules, to assure that you are doing everything possible to allow your system to perform as it has historically. If you don't follow the rules, then both the conditions — the market's behavior and your system — become variables.

With this understanding, before you trade your system, there are three questions (which also apply to a hotline service) that you should ask yourself:

1. **What is my system's drawdown?**

2. **How much money do I need to trade my system?**

3. **What money management strategy will I use to trade my system?**

Know the dollar size of your system's drawdown so that you can determine how much money you will need to trade your system and whether or not you can afford to trade the system. To determine the dollar amount, take the system's drawdown amount and double it. Add this dollar amount to a base dollar amount. The resulting sum should be large enough to absorb losses equivalent to twice the system's drawdown, leaving you with enough capital to continue to trade according to your system's money management strategy. Account equity of this size or larger is considered to be adequate capitalization for a given system.

ACCOUNT CAPITALIZATION AND MONEY MANAGEMENT

You can double all of the money in your trading account many times, but lose it all only once. Next to trading discipline, money management is the single most important factor in determining your success as a trader. Spend some time researching this subject and choose a strategy before you begin trading. My approach is to keep it simple with regard to money management.

One of my mentors, Larry Williams, has presented the most effective, straightforward approach to money management I have seen to date. He uses a ratio of equity risk percentage to stop dollar amount to determine the number of contracts to risk on any one trade. The formula is:

$$\text{\# of contracts to trade} = \frac{\text{risk \% } \times \text{ account equity}}{\text{trade stop dollar amount}}$$

In this formula, the risk percentage should range from 5% to 25%. A 20% equity risk is aggressive. A 5% to 10% risk is conservative. I have traded beyond 25% at times, but in practical terms of risk management (and restful nights), an equity risk of 20% or less is where most individuals should be trading. As an illustration of this point, consider the three plots in Chart 2.1, which show the same 25 trades given three different risk percentages: 10%, 20%, and 30%.

> **"Next to trading discipline, money management is the single most important factor in determining your success as a trader."**

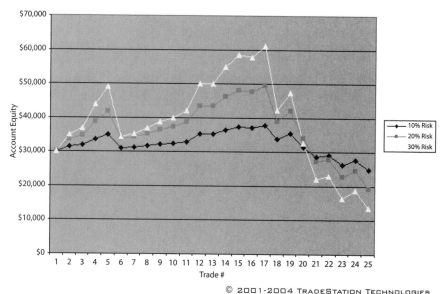

CHART 2.1   THREE RISK PERCENTAGES IN ACTION

The beginning account size is $30,000 and a $1,300 stop order was used on each trade. The price data used to generate each curve was identical, taken from the real-time application of a Treasury bond system that I trade. The curve includes a drawdown period. The 30% risk percentage showed the steepest growth curve, but it also generated unacceptable losses during the system's drawdown period. At the peak of the 30% risk curve, the account size was doubled, but at the end of the drawdown, the 30% risk percentage generated losses of nearly 80% of this peak value with an ending equity balance of $13,000 at the close of the drawdown. In comparison, the 20% risk percentage generated an equity dip of about 60%, based on $50,000 at the peak of the growth curve to about $20,000 at the end of the drawdown. The 10% risk percentage sustained losses of about 30% of account equity, from $38,000 at the peak of the growth curve to about $27,000 at the bottom of the drawdown.

The message here is that there is a "sweet spot" among the risk percentages in the money management formula. You want to trade a risk percentage that is large enough to generate strong equity growth, but one that is not so large that the drawdown represents an unwieldy percentage of your equity — such as the case of the 30% risk percentage that resulted in an 80% drawdown. In general, a risk percentage between

10% and 20% is the place for you to be. For new traders, I would recommend 5% to 10% for the first couple of years.

Once you have chosen an equity percentage in the 5% to 20% range, stick with it. Do not adjust your risk percentage by trade. Consider Tables 2.1 and 2.2. Each represents the same 25 trades that were used in Chart 2.1, beginning with an account balance of $30,000 and using a $1,300 stop on each trade. In Table 2.1, I have selected the risk percentage at random on any given trade. In Table 2.2, I have applied a consistent 15% equity risk on each trade.

Random Equity Risk Percentage	Number of contracts to trade	Single Contract P&L	P&L with Random use of Money Management Formula Risk Percentage	Account Balance
20	5	$726.78	$3,634	$30,000
10	3	$226.78	$680	$33,634
15	4	$789.28	$3,157	$34,314
10	3	$508.03	$1,524	$37,471
20	6	-$1,335.72	-$8,014	$38,995
20	5	$101.78	$509	$30,981
10	2	$195.53	$391	$31,490
15	4	$258.03	$1,032	$31,881
15	4	$133.03	$532	$32,913
20	5	$226.78	$1,134	$33,445
10	3	$789.28	$2,368	$34,579
10	3	$8.03	$24	$36,947
15	4	$414.28	$1,657	$36,971
20	6	$258.03	$1,548	$38,628
10	3	-$54.47	-$163	$40,176
10	3	$258.03	$774	$40,013
20	6	-$1,335.72	-$8,014	$40,787
20	5	$508.03	$2,540	$32,773
10	3	-$1,335.72	-$4,007	$35,313
20	5	-$1,335.72	-$6,679	$31,306
10	2	$195.53	$391	$24,627
15	3	-$1,335.72	-$4,007	$25,018
20	3	$633.03	$1,899	$21,011
15	3	-$1,335.72	-$4,007	$22,910

Final account balance @ random risk % **$22,910**

TABLE 2.1 $30,000 ACCOUNT TRADED WITH RANDOM EQUITY RISK PERCENTAGE

Consistent 15% Equity Risk Percentage	Number of contracts to trade	Single Contract P&L	P&L with Consistent use of Money Management Formula Risk Percentage at 15%	Account Balance
15	3	$726.78	$2,180	$30,000
15	4	$226.78	$907	$32,180
15	4	$789.28	$3,157	$33,087
15	4	$508.03	$2,032	$36,245
15	4	-$1,335.72	-$5,343	$38,277
15	4	$101.78	$407	$32,934
15	4	$195.53	$782	$33,341
15	4	$258.03	$1,032	$34,123
15	4	$133.03	$532	$35,155
15	4	$226.78	$907	$35,687
15	4	$789.28	$3,157	$36,594
15	5	$8.03	$40	$39,752
15	5	$414.28	$2,071	$39,792
15	5	$258.03	$1,290	$41,863
15	5	-$54.47	-$272	$43,153
15	5	$258.03	$1,290	$42,881
15	5	-$1,335.72	-$6,679	$44,171
15	4	$508.03	$2,032	$37,492
15	5	-$1,335.72	-$6,679	$39,525
15	4	-$1,335.72	-$5,343	$32,846
15	3	$195.53	$587	$27,503
15	3	-$1,335.72	-$4,007	$28,090
15	3	$633.03	$1,899	$24,083
15	3	-$1,335.72	-$4,007	$25,982

Final account balance @ 15 risk %   **$25,982**

TABLE 2.2 $30,000 ACCOUNT TRADED WITH CONSISTENT 15% EQUITY RISK PERCENTAGE

Note that the final account balance is greater with a consistent 15% risk applied. This is a simple example, but the lesson here is to find a risk percentage in your money management strategy that you are comfortable with and apply it consistently on each trade. Over time, this approach will start to make more money than a random application of the same risk percentage.

In the preceeding pages of this chapter, I have outlined a guide for you to follow in our preparations to trade or improve your current trading ability: know yourself; know winning traders; know your trading style and market; know discipline and money management; and have a system. Time spent upfront understanding and employing these guidelines will improve your odds for successful trading.

DEVELOPING YOUR OWN TRADING SYSTEM

Working through my losses and back to a more viable trading program convinced me of the importance for traders to develop and trade their own systems. But where do you start? There are as many different kinds of systems and ways to trade them as there are traders. There are also a number of areas in which to develop and apply a system — futures, options on futures, spreads, arbitrage scenarios, and so forth. My comments on system development are based on my experience with short-term trading in the 30-year Treasury bond market, but the basic principles are applicable to all markets.

To develop a short-term system, it is common to test the past in order to predict the future. A typical short-term trading system is a theoretical model of future market behavior built upon past market conditions or "filters" and a set of trading rules for each condition. The short-term system is comprised of any number of these sorts of market conditions, as many as the system developer cares to consider. Thus, the system developer selects a particular market condition — such as the inter-day price relationship between two price bars — and a set of trading rules for the condition, and then filters a set of historical price data. (I use about 12 years of data in the 30-year bond market.)

When the market condition filter and trading rules applied to this price data forecast a clear market direction for future market behavior, the system developer adds this filter and the corresponding trading rules to the system model. This process is repeated with any number and type of filters until the developer is satisfied that the model represents a reasonable spectrum of market conditions. Each trading day, the system developer/trader compares the current market conditions to the specific market conditions that comprise the system's model. When there is a match, the system generates a trade.

System Development in Action

Here's an example of how the development process might work. The first step is to select filters — one technical and one fundamental — from the choices below. Then, general trade entry and exit rules must be determined. The final step is to apply the selected filters and trade rules to a set of historical price data and examine the results. I consider three categories of market condition filters in developing my own short-term trading systems: technical, fundamental, and a combination of both.

Technical filters include (among other things):

■ **Inter-day price relationships between the opening, high, low, and closing prices of a one-day session relative to that of the prior.**

■ **Moving averages.**

■ **Momentum indicators.**

■ **"Accumulation indexes," which are indexes that quantify a market's accumulation of buying or selling.**

For example, I will use the inter-day price relationships for our technical filters.

Fundamental market condition filters include:

■ **Trading Day Of the Week (TDOW), which is one of my favorites. This is a very simple and useful filter that I first learned from Larry Williams.**

■ **Commercial and public sentiment numbers.**

As with the technical filters, there are many fundamental filters and plenty of room for creativity in their application. For our example, I will use TDOW.

The **market entry rules** include three different order types: market, limit and stop. A market order is an order to buy or sell at the current market price. A limit order is placed below the current market for a buy and above the current market for a sell. A limit order to buy would be filled if the market first sold off from its current price down to a price at or below the limit order price. A stop order is the inverse of a limit order. With a stop order, we buy above the current market price and sell below it. For example, a stop order to buy is an order to buy at a price above the current market price. In order to fill a stop order, the market must first rally up to a price at or above the stop order price.

The order entry to use is one that maximizes profits and minimizes losses. In this regard, the order type (or entry rule) selected will vary from one market condition to the next. In this example, for the sake of simplicity, we will use a market order entry rule.

The market exit rule I also use almost exclusively, and which I use in this example, is First Profitable Open (FPO), which I learned from Larry Williams. The FPO rule states that a trade position is held until the first market open that is profitable to our position or until we get stopped out or reverse position, whichever comes first. Always trade with stops. With every trade, work an open protective stop order opposite the position. If the market moves through this protective stop order before the trade turns profitable, the trade is exited on a stop loss.

Here's a review of my system example:

- **For filters, I use inter-day price relationships (technical) and TDOW (fundamental). I believe the systems that hold up best over time are those that employ both technical and fundamentals filters.**
- **For my trade entry rule, I use a market order.**
- **My trade exit rule is First Profitable Open (FPO).**

The next thing to do, is apply these filters and trading rules to historical price data. Our example uses 12 years of price data in the 30-year Treasury bond markets (1990 to 2002).

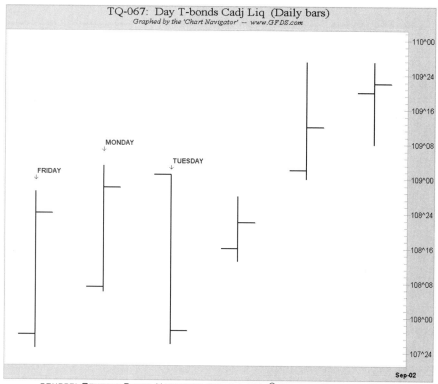

CHART 2.2 **PRICE BARS USED AS TECHNICAL FILTERS IN T-BOND SYSTEM.**

As Chart 2.2 shows, we used our technical filter to examine the inter-day relationship between Monday's bar and Friday's bar. (This is only one of many inter-day price relationships that can be used as technical filter criteria.) Compared with Friday, Monday's open was less than Friday's close; Monday's low was above Friday's low, and its close was above Friday's high. Now, we examine our 12 years of Treasury bond price data in the Treasury bond market. I want to determine how well, for each trading day of the week (our fundamental filter), a trade performs when we buy every market open (my market order-entry rule) that matches the inter-day price relationship criteria (my technical filter), exit first profitable open, and use an open $1,300 protective sell stop order opposite our position.

Buy Signal Performance by TDOW					
	M	T	W	Th	F	TDOW Totals
# of Trades	36	26	34	34	26	156
# of Wins	26	25	25	27	20	123
# of Loss	10	1	9	7	6	33
Accuracy	72.22%	96.15%	73.53%	79.41%	76.92%	78.85%
APPT	-$158.88	$429.76	-$91.87	$64.00	-$10.13	$27.20
Total Prof.	-$5,719.70	$11,173.80	-$3,123.70	$2,176.00	-$263.50	$4,242.90

TABLE 2.3   TRADE PERFORMANCE USING INTER-DAY
PRICE RELATIONSHIPS AND TDOW FILTER.

In the 12 years of data, the criteria for the technical filter was met 156 times. The results of this filter alone are nothing to speak of: an Average Profit Per Trade (APPT) of $27.20 and a trade accuracy of 78.85%. But if you look at this filter along with the TDOW filter, you'll see something interesting. As Table 2.3 shows, trades on a Tuesday were profitable 96.15% of the time on 26 trades in the past 12 years. The APPT was $429.76. These are the kinds of results that we look for in developing a reliable system. It also would be a specific market condition that you would probably want to add to your system model so that when market conditions match these conditions (Monday/Friday inter-day price relationship), your system will tell that if the TDOW is a Tuesday, look to buy the market at the open, exit FPO, and work an open $1,300 sell stop order.

After adding these market conditions and trading rules to the model, the system developer/trader would then continue to filter price data with different market conditions, looking for trade results with the strength of those in Table 2.3. The conditions that successfully met the criteria would then be added to the system model. When the developer is satisfied with the number of market conditions integrated into the model, the system should be complete and ready to trade.

System development is a creative process that requires a good deal of critical thinking and can be very rewarding for those who like to "get under the hood and get their hands dirty." Personally, I like the level of control that developing and trading my own systems gives me. It allows me to be on top of what I'm doing in trading and why.

My own experience has taught me that there is only one sure thing in trading: There are no shortcuts to a successful trading career. As I look back on my education in the markets — from early losses and blown out trading accounts to winning the World Cup — it is clear that many lessons can only be learned first-hand, but it is my hope that the lessons I have chronicled in this chapter will help you to find the direction and inspiration you need to improve your personal bottom line as you build your own successful trading career.

PART 2

THE SYSTEMATIC TRADER

Wanting to trade and becoming successful at it are two entirely different things. In fact, these two phases of trading can be light years apart, separated by months or even years of losses, frustration and fear. As we saw in the first section, the difference between those who trade and those who become consistently successful at it, often comes down to one thing: **a system**. Whether a customized approach or an off-the-shelf model, trading systems go a long way to eliminate one of the most volatile and unpredictable elements in trading: human nature.

Over the years, I've seen many traders lose it all because they believed they were "in tune" or "in sync" with the market. They relied on instincts instead of indicators. Instead of studying market patterns of the past, they tried to determine the future by their gut-feelings. This approach to trading is almost always a recipe for disaster. The problem is that the market happens in real-time. While the market plays out — tick-for-tick — a host of human emotions come into play: fear, greed, hope, doubt, anger, elation and impatience, just to name a few. You can go from certainty to second-guessing yourself in an instant.

The only way to eliminate those human emotions is with a trading system. Based on a particular set of parameters, determined and thoroughly tested using historical data, a trading system provides a detailed strategy. It indicates with a much higher degree of reliability where to get in and where to get out, how much to risk per trade and where to put a stop. Trading systems can be as simple or as complicated as a trader/developer wishes.

Over the years, I've seen an array of systems, including some very good ones and some that were notably bad. What each of these systems had in common, however, was the ability to make trades based on specific criteria. Systems allow traders to turn their best ideas, observations and beliefs about market behavior into hypotheses that are back tested to determine theoretical performance. When the conditions have been tested and the parameters are set, the systems are ready to trade live. The system then filters real-time data through the "screens" of the specified criteria: for example market movement, timeframe, day of the week, and so forth. When the criteria are met, a trade happens. If one of the criteria is not met, there is no trade.

How to develop, test and implement a system are common questions for most traders. If you've ever asked these questions, you're about to get the education you've longed for! In the next three chapters, three World Cup Champions — Neil Peplinski, Chuck Hughes and Kurt Sakaeda — explain in detail and great depth the development of their systems that led to their championship returns. For any trader, a look "over the shoulder" of these notable traders is a valuable experience.

Human nature being what it is, there is the constant temptation to override even the best trading system on the often unfounded belief that a trader knows more than the system. Yet, the best system traders know — usually from their own hard-knocks — that it takes discipline to develop, implement and stick with a system.

As Peplinski, the 1998 winner (non-professional division) of the *World Cup Championship* observes, "Following a trading plan exactly is very difficult. The human element — fear, greed, doubt, second-guessing, relying on hunches — can get in the way of even the best designed and most thoroughly tested system."

Peplinski, a Commodity Trading Advisor in the Chicago area, describes his calculated approach to the markets with systems that "would tell me exactly where to enter a trade and exactly when to get out." The systems he developed helped him leap to the front of the competitive trading crowd with a 95% return on his first appearance in the *World Cup Championship*. He came very close (a 4.35% margin) to topping all competitors that year.

While his return is impressive, in his chapter Peplinski evaluates the actual trades from his championship run, an exercise that yields a startling discovery — and an important lesson. While a devoted systematic trader, he did not completely remove the human element from his trading, which (at least theoretically) may have kept this first-place winner from turning in an even *better* performance. For traders who are tempted to over-ride their systems on occasion, this is a candid reminder of the potential returns they could be passing up.

Weighing in next is Hughes, the 1999 winner (professional division) of the *World Cup Championship*. Step-by-step, Hughes lays out how traders and developers back test and implement systems that have a long history of success — instead of trying to guess future price movements. His advice is certainly worth heeding: Hughes won the 1999 World Cup in a hotly contested year that saw three accounts appreciate more than 100%. His 315% return captured the overall title that year and earned him his fourth trophy since first competing in the *World Cup Trading Championships* in 1994.

Many of the best traders in the world were — at one time — also avid gamblers. The techniques they perfected to count cards and evaluate their risk on every hand also had broad applications for the trading markets. Kurt Sakaeda follows in this tradition. By combining his love of gambling and trading, Sakaeda developed a unique Seasonal Trading System that helps him hone in on the highest-potential trades while identifying when to sidestep an opportunity patiently. His unique approach to timing the market is made even more accessible to all traders with the advent of today's inexpensive computers and software programs.

Reading how these three championship traders developed, tested and implemented a trading system will be a valuable education to all traders, from the novice exploring trading methodologies to the more experienced looking to fine-tune their own systems. A trading system alone will not guarantee a trader's success. Indeed, much still depends upon the quality and reliability of the system as well as a trader's discipline in following it. Without a system, however, it becomes far more difficult to trade with consistency and confidence.

CHAPTER 3

Rules of the Trade: Developing a Winning Trading System

By Neil Peplinski

For many traders, the difference between success and failure in the market comes down to one essential element: developing and following a trading plan. In my own career, I've seen the startling evidence of what a trading plan can do. Before I undertook a systematic approach to trading, I suffered losses that virtually wiped out my accounts. I was undercapitalized. I had no clear idea of how much money I needed, how much I should risk per trade, or what kind of profit I needed to generate to stay in the game.

Once I set my goal on arriving at a calculated approach to the markets, I focused on developing a system that would tell me exactly when to enter a trade — and exactly when to get out. In time, I was able to develop a winning trading system, which ultimately allowed me to win the *Robbins' World Cup Championship of Futures Trading*.

My goal in this chapter is to show you how to develop and implement a winning trading system. The markets you choose, your own style of trading, and the indicators and parameters that work the best for you will all be part of the system and strategy you ultimately embrace. Just as I began my education by familiarizing myself with the work of numerous other mechanical traders, learning from their experience, trials and tribulations, I believe my experience will also be educational and insightful to others.

It took about a year of research and work to develop my own system. After that, I reached the point at which I was ready to place orders again. This time my hard work paid off: I posted a 190% return in one trading account and a 141% return in another. With a renewed commitment to trade and confidence in my own ability, I set my sights on the next challenge: the *World Cup Championship*. From the start, I took a very systematic approach to what appeared at the beginning to be a very daunting task. I started with the parameters that I knew: The minimum account size was $10,000 and there was a $1,000 entry fee. I had decided to commit $15,000 to the effort. Minus the $1,000 fee, that left me with a starting account size of $14,000.

Once my capitalization was determined, the next step was to find markets that had a good mix of volatility to offer some significant short-term price movements and liquidity. I was targeting techniques that used a one- to five-day holding period and had multiple transactions per month so that enough trades would be generated throughout the course of the year. I feared that systems that only traded once a month or less would not provide enough opportunities to realize a winning return. In addition, given the starting account size, it was also important to consider margin requirements.

In the end, I settled upon 30-Year Treasury bonds, coffee and the New York Futures Exchange (NYFE) with margins at the time of $2,700, $9,800 and $5,500 respectively. I had considered the Dow Jones Industrial Average and S&P 500 as potential indices, but settled upon the NYFE. Dow futures were only a few months old at the time and were still light on liquidity. The S&P 500 offered the same profit potential as the NYFE, but at the time they had more than twice the margin. *(Note: Since then, liquidity in the NYFE has dropped substantially and I believe this market is no longer a viable trading option).*

The next step in my systematic approach was to research and compile specific trading rules that would match both my account size and the types of markets that I would trade. Some of the concepts that I will discuss in this chapter — which I used in my competitive account — were original ideas. Many were based on previously published ideas I adapted to my own style.

For all three markets, I deducted $100 per trade for slippage and commissions. Being an advocate of stop-loss orders, I elected to use a $2,500 stop in the NYFE, a $1,375 stop in bonds, and a $1,500 stop in coffee. As I developed the systems to trade, an essential element would be back testing. To do this, I used test data from 1982 through 1997, including several subintervals (1982–1988, 1989–1997, 1982–1987, 1987–1992, 1992–1997) to see how each rule responded to different market conditions (bull, bear and sideways). Only rules that were profitable in all timeframes would be used.

NYFE SIGNALS

I used a total of five entry triggers for the NYFE market:

- OPTION EXPIRATION
- OUTSIDE DOWN CLOSE
- CLUE!
- FIRST/LAST WEEK
- INSIDE UP CLOSE

Option Expiration: I first learned about the option expiration trade while reading the works of Larry Williams. The option expiration trade is based on the concept that the stock market typically rallies during the days leading up to the expiration of stock options. It also uses an exit technique made popular by Williams that calls for exiting the trade on the first profitable close. This exit technique is highly effective and is used by a number of short-term traders including myself.

Rule: Buy the close on the Friday before option expiration. Typically, this means buying on the close of the second Friday of the month. Exit using a $2,500 stop or on the first profitable close.

Performance Summary: Long Trades			
Total net profit	$47,625.00	Open position P/L	$0.00
Gross profit	$68,800.00	Gross loss	–$21,175.00
Total # of trades	121	Percent profitable	86%
Number winning trades	104	Number losing trades	17
Largest winning trade	$4,800.00	Largest losing trade	–$2,600.00
Average winning trade	$661.54	Average losing trade	–$1,245.59
Ratio avg. win/avg. loss	0.53	Avg. trade(win & loss)	$393.60
Max consec. winners	22	Max consec. losers	2
Avg. # bars in winners	2	Avg. # bars in losers	3
Max intraday drawdown	–$6,600.00		
Profit factor	3.25	Max # contracts held	1

Test Period	Trades	Net Profit	Avg. Trade	Profit Factor	Drawdown
1982-1988	52	$6,050	$116	1.46	($6,600)
1989-1997	68	$41,500	$610	6.19	($3,200)
1982-1987	44	$1,825	$41	1.14	($6,600)
1987-1992	46	$23,725	$516	9.63	($4,375)
1992-1997	45	$24,825	$552	4.12	($3,2300)

RESULTS: OPTION EXPIRATION
05/06/82 – 12/26/97

Outside Down Close: An outside day occurs when the high is higher than the previous day's high and the low is lower than the previous day's low. In stock index futures, this type of price action can have a bullish tendency. Actually, as we'll see later, it is effective in other markets as well.

Rule: If today is an outside day with a close lower than yesterday's close and tomorrow opens below today's close, buy tomorrow at today's close on a stop. Exit using a $2,500 stop or on the first profitable open.

Performance Summary: Long Trades			
Total net profit	$32,375.00	Open position P/L	$0.00
Gross profit	$46,075.00	Gross loss	–$13,700.00
Total # of trades	92	Percent profitable	82%
Number winning trades	75	Number losing trades	17
Largest winning trade	$2,875.00	Largest losing trade	–$2,600.00
Average winning trade	$614.33	Average losing trade	–$805.88
Ratio avg. win/avg. loss	0.76	Avg. trade(win & loss)	$351.90
Max consec. winners	15	Max consec. losers	3
Av # bars in winners	1	Avg. # bars in losers	3
Max intraday drawdown	–$4,575.00		
Profit factor	3.36	Max # contracts held	1

Test Period	Trades	Net Profit	Avg. Trade	Profit Factor	Drawdown
1982-1988	36	$14,575	$405	3.60	($4,575)
1989-1997	56	$17,800	$318	3.20	($3,550)
1982-1987	27	$6,975	$258	2.28	($4,575)
1987-1992	37	$19,625	$530	8.07	($3,550)
1992-1997	40	$12,450	$311	3.27	($3025)

RESULTS: OUTSIDE DAY DOWN CLOSE
05/06/82 – 12/26/97

CLUE!: The next signal was one I affectionately call CLUE!, which stands for Close Low Under Extreme. (It seems to me that all good trading signals have a catchy name, so I thought it was appropriate.) CLUE! looks to buy on a rally after a short-term correction.

Rule: If today's close is below yesterday's low (an extreme close) and tomorrow opens down and tomorrow is not a Thursday or Friday, then buy tomorrow at today's close. Exit using a $2,500 stop or on the first profitable open.

Performance Summary: Long Trades			
Total net profit	$67,000.00	Open position P/L	$0.00
Gross profit	$88,875.00	Gross loss	-$21,875.00
Total # of trades	149	Percent profitable	81%
Number winning trades	121	Number losing trades	28
Largest winning trade	$14,825.00	Largest losing trade	-$2,600.00
Average winning trade	$734.50	Average losing trade	-$781.25
Ratio avg. win/avg. loss	0.94	Avg. trade(win & loss)	$449.66
Max consec. winners	17	Max consec. losers	3
Av # bars in winners	2	Avg. # bars in losers	3
Max intraday drawdown	-$4,625.00		
Profit factor	4.06	Max # contracts held	1

Test Period	Trades	Net Profit	Avg. Trade	Profit Factor	Drawdown
1982-1988	70	$14,225	$203	2.27	($4,625)
1989-1997	79	$52,775	$668	5.93	($3,725)
1982-1987	59	$8,325	$141	1.76	($4,625)
1987-1992	66	$34,175	$518	12.02	($3,275)
1992-1997	44	$35,300	$802	5.43	($3,725)

RESULTS: CLUE! (CLOSE LOW UNDER EXTREME)
05/06/82 – 12/26/97

First/Last Week: This trading signal was designed to take advantage of the upward bias in the stock market at the beginning and end of each month.

Rule: If tomorrow is the first trading day of the week and the calendar date is between the 1st and the 4th of the month or the 29th or later, buy tomorrow's open plus 10% of today's range. The exit is a $2,500 stop or the first profitable open.

Performance Summary: Long Trades			
Total net profit	$70,475.00	Open position P/L	$0.00
Gross profit	$94,800.00	Gross loss	–$24,325.00
Total # of trades	140	Percent profitable	89%
Number winning trades	124	Number losing trades	16
Largest winning trade	$5,650.00	Largest losing trade	–$3,150.00
Average winning trade	$764.52	Average losing trade	–$1,520.31
Ratio avg. win/avg. loss	0.50	Avg. trade(win & loss)	$503.39
Max consec. winners	32	Max consec. losers	3
Avg. # bars in winners	2	Avg. # bars in losers	4
Max intraday drawdown	–$5,850.00		
Profit factor	3.90	Max # contracts held	1

Test Period	Trades	Net Profit	Avg. Trade	Profit Factor	Drawdown
1982-1988	52	$18,075	$348	3.22	($5,850)
1989-1997	87	$51,375	$591	4.18	($3,750)
1982-1987	44	$10,575	$240	2.30	($5,850)
1987-1992	57	$36,400	$639	5.65	($3,750)
1992-1997	57	$33,600	$590	4.06	($3,675)

RESULTS: FIRST/LAST WEEK BIAS
05/06/82 – 12/26/97

BOND SIGNALS

In the 30-Year Treasury Bond market, I used a total of three entry triggers:

- **PROJECTED OOPS!**
- **OUTSIDE DOWN CLOSE**
- **WEEKEND BOND GETAWAY**

Projected OOPS!: Similar to the options expiration trade in the NYFE, the Projected OOPS! signal is based on a popular signal created by Williams called OOPS!. My version incorporates tomorrow's projected low, which is calculated as follows:

$$\text{Tomorrow's Projected Low} = \frac{(\text{High} + \text{Low} + \text{Close})}{3 \times 2 - \text{High}}$$

Rule: If Monday opens below the larger of Friday's low or Monday's projected low, buy at the smaller of Friday's low or Monday's projected low. Exit using a $1,375 stop or on the first profitable open after holding the trade for at least two days.

Performance Summary: Long Trades			
Total net profit	$53,968.75	Open position P/L	$0.00
Gross profit	$83,043.75	Gross loss	−$29,075.00
Total # of trades	125	Percent profitable	78%
Number winning trades	98	Number losing trades	27
Largest winning trade	$6,775.00	Largest losing trade	−$1,975.00
Average winning trade	$847.39	Average losing trade	−$1,076.85
Ratio avg. win/avg. loss	0.79	Avg. trade(win & loss)	$431.75
Max consec. winners	13	Max consec. losers	3
Avg. # bars in winners	4	Avg. # bars in losers	4
Max intraday drawdown	−$4,700.00		
Profit factor	2.86	Max # contracts held	1

Test Period	Trades	Net Profit	Avg. Trade	Profit Factor	Drawdown
1982-1988	65	$30,156	$464	2.62	($4,700)
1989-1997	60	$23,813	$397	3.28	($2,513)
1982-1987	58	$30,856	$532	2.81	($4,700)
1987-1992	42	$14,863	$354	2.55	($3,319)
1992-1997	39	$15,100	$387	2.71	($2,038)

RESULTS: PROJECTED OOPS!
01/04/82 − 12/26/97

Outside Down Close: This signal is very similar to the method that worked in the NYFE market and again makes note of an outside day.

Rule: If today is an outside day with a close less than yesterday's close, then buy tomorrow at the open plus 20% of today's range. Exit using a $1,375 stop or on the first profitable open after holding the trade for at least one full market day.

Performance Summary: Long Trades			
Total net profit	$43,368.75	Open position P/L	$0.00
Gross profit	$69,350.00	Gross loss	–$25,981.25
Total # of trades	136	Percent profitable	80%
Number winning trades	109	Number losing trades	27
Largest winning trade	$2,400.00	Largest losing trade	–$1,756.25
Average winning trade	$636.24	Average losing trade	–$962.27
Ratio avg. win/avg. loss	0.66	Avg. trade(win & loss)	$318.89
Max consec. winners	19	Max consec. losers	4
Avg. # bars in winners	3	Avg. # bars in losers	3
Max intraday drawdown	–$5,768.75		
Profit factor	2.67	Max # contracts held	1

Test Period	Trades	Net Profit	Avg. Trade	Profit Factor	Drawdown
1982-1988	57	$20,956	$368	2.51	($5,769)
1989-1997	79	$22,413	$284	2.85	($5,663)
1982-1987	49	$17,288	$353	2.25	($5,013)
1987-1992	54	$10,038	$186	1.91	($5,763)
1992-1997	44	$12,881	$293	2.73	($3,975)

RESULTS: OUTSIDE DOWN CLOSE
01/04/82 – 12/26/97

Weekend Bond Getaway: This signal works for both long and short trades and looks to enter on Friday to hold a position over the weekend when most short-term traders are on the sidelines. The buy setup is strength on Thursday but a weaker Friday open. The sell setup is weakness on Thursday but with a stronger open on Friday.

Rule: If today is Thursday and the market closes above yesterday's high and tomorrow's open is between today's low and today's close, buy tomorrow at today's close on a stop. The sell side works just the opposite. If today is Thursday and the market closes below yesterday's low and tomorrow's open is between today's high and today's close, sell tomorrow at today's close on a stop. Exit using a $1,375 stop or on the first profitable open. Also use a 50% trailing stop with a $500 floor. (When profits reach $500, move the stop up to protect 50% of the open position profits. If the market continues to move favorably, move the stop accordingly.)

Performance Summary: All Trades			
Total net profit	$31,443.75	Open position P/L	$0.00
Gross profit	$51,387.50	Gross loss	–$19,943.75
Total # of trades	129	Percent profitable	76%
Number winning trades	98	Number losing trades	31
Largest winning trade	$2,400.00	Largest losing trade	–$1,568.75
Average winning trade	$524.36	Average losing trade	–$643.35
Ratio avg. win/avg. loss	0.82	Avg. trade(win & loss)	$243.75
Max consec. winners	16	Max consec. losers	3
Avg. # bars in winners	1	Avg. # bars in losers	2
Max intraday drawdown	–$3,387.50		
Profit factor	2.58	Max # contracts held	1

Performance Summary: Long Trades			
Total net profit	$15,131.25	Open position P/L	$0.00
Gross profit	$25,906.25	Gross loss	–$10,775.00
Total # of trades	64	Percent profitable	70%
Number winning trades	45	Number losing trades	19
Largest winning trade	$2,025.00	Largest losing trade	–$1,475.00
Average winning trade	$575.69	Average losing trade	–$567.11
Ratio avg. win/avg. loss	1.02	Avg. trade(win & loss)	$236.43
Max consec. winners	8	Max consec. losers	4
Avg. # bars in winners	1	Avg. # bars in losers	2
Max intraday drawdown	–$3,850.00		
Profit factor	2.40	Max # contracts held	1

Performance Summary: Short Trades			
Total net profit	$16,312.50	Open position P/L	$0.00
Gross profit	$25,481.25	Gross loss	–$9,168.75
Total # of trades	65	Percent profitable	82%
Number winning trades	53	Number losing trades	12
Largest winning trade	$2,400.00	Largest losing trade	–$1568.75
Average winning trade	$480.78	Average losing trade	–$764.06
Ratio avg. win/avg. loss	0.63	Avg. trade(win & loss)	$250.96
Max consec. winners	16	Max consec. losers	2
Avg. # bars in winners	2	Avg. # bars in losers	2
Max intraday drawdown	–$2,887.50		
Profit factor	2.78	Max # contracts held	1

Test Period	Trades	Net Profit	Avg. Trade	Profit Factor	Drawdown
1982-1988	38	$5,013	$132	1.54	($3,388)
1989-1997	91	$26,431	$290	3.48	($3031)
1982-1987	36	$6,525	$181	1.84	($3,388)
1987-1992	44	$10,225	$232	2.69	($3,269)
1992-1997	63	$19,294	$306	3.51	($3,031)

RESULTS: WEEKEND BOND GETAWAY
01/04/82 – 12/26/97

Coffee Signals

In the coffee market, I used just two signals, both of which provided buy and sell orders.

■ COOPS!   ■ FAKE OUT

COOPS!: Similar to Williams' OOPS! signal, COOPS! buys or sells at the previous day's close instead of the previous day's low or high.

Rule: If today's high is below yesterday's high and today's low is above yesterday's low (an inside day), and tomorrow opens below today's low or down at least one full point, then buy tomorrow at today's close on a stop. On the sell side, if we have an inside day and tomorrow opens above today's high or up at least one full point, then sell tomorrow at today's close. Exit using a $1,500 stop or on the close the day after entry regardless of profit or loss.

Performance Summary: All Trades			
Total net profit	$72,601.25	Open position P/L	$881.25
Gross profit	$102,373.75	Gross loss	−$29,772.50
Total # of trades	112	Percent profitable	63%
Number winning trades	71	Number losing trades	41
Largest winning trade	$14,412.50	Largest losing trade	−$2,387.50
Average winning trade	$1,441.88	Average losing trade	−$726.16
Ratio avg. win/avg. loss	1.99	Avg. trade(win & loss)	$648.23
Max consec. winners	9	Max consec. losers	3
Avg. # bars in winners	1	Avg. # bars in losers	1
Max intraday drawdown	−$4,376.25		
Profit factor	3.44	Max # contracts held	1

Performance Summary: Long Trades			
Total net profit	$42,357.50	Open position P/L	$0.00
Gross profit	$60,678.75	Gross loss	−$18,321.25
Total # of trades	64	Percent profitable	66%
Number winning trades	42	Number losing trades	22
Largest winning trade	$14,412.50	Largest losing trade	−$2,387.50
Average winning trade	$1,444.73	Average losing trade	−$832.78
Ratio avg. win/avg. loss	1.73	Avg. trade(win & loss)	$661.84
Max consec. winners	6	Max consec. losers	4
Avg. # bars in winners	1	Avg. # bars in losers	1
Max intraday drawdown	−$3,850.00		
Profit factor	2.40	Max # contracts held	1

Performance Summary: Short Trades			
Total net profit	$30,243.75	Open position P/L	$881.25
Gross profit	$41,695.00	Gross loss	–$11,451.25
Total # of trades	48	Percent profitable	60%
Number winning trades	29	Number losing trades	19
Largest winning trade	$6,518.75	Largest losing trade	–$1,678.75
Average winning trade	$1,437.76	Average losing trade	–$602.70
Ratio avg. win/avg. loss	2.39	Avg. trade(win & loss)	$630.08
Max consec. winners	5	Max consec. losers	3
Avg. # bars in winners	1	Avg. # bars in losers	1
Max intraday drawdown	–$3,476.25		
Profit factor	3.64	Max # contracts held	1

Test Period	Trades	Net Profit	Avg. Trade	Profit Factor	Drawdown
1982-1988	53	$13,315	$251	2.37	($4,376)
1989-1997	59	$59,286	$1005	3.96	($3,988)
1982-1987	42	$11,516	$274	2.48	($4,376)
1987-1992	44	$13,994	$318	3.33	($1,919)
1992-1997	39	$53,400	$1369	4.15	($3,988)

RESULTS: COOPS! 01/04/82 – 12/31/97

Fake Out: A fake-out day is one that has a lower low than the previous day but then closes higher (or a higher high than the previous day with a lower close). After this counter-close the market often continues in the direction prior to the fake out. This presents some great short-term opportunities, especially in coffee.

Rule: If today's low is less than yesterday's low and today's close is higher than yesterday's close and tomorrow opens above today's low, then sell tomorrow at today's low on a stop. If today's high is greater than yesterday's high and today's close is less than yesterday's close and today's close is greater than the close five days ago and tomorrow opens less than today's high, buy tomorrow at today's high on a stop. Exit using a $1,500 stop or on the first profitable open.

Performance Summary: All Trades

Total net profit	$50,963.75	Open position P/L	$0.00
Gross profit	$77,041.25	Gross loss	−$26,077.50
Total # of trades	118	Percent profitable	75%
Number winning trades	88	Number losing trades	30
Largest winning trade	$5,337.50	Largest losing trade	−$1,817.50
Average winning trade	$875.47	Average losing trade	−$869.25
Ratio avg. win/avg. loss	1.01	Avg. trade(win & loss)	$648.23
Max consec. winners	8	Max consec. losers	3
Avg. # bars in winners	2	Avg. # bars in losers	2
Max intraday drawdown	−$3,812.50		
Profit factor	2.95	Max # contracts held	1

Performance Summary: Long Trades

Total net profit	$13,492.50	Open position P/L	$0.00
Gross profit	$22,458.75	Gross loss	−$8,966.25
Total # of trades	54	Percent profitable	72%
Number winning trades	39	Number losing trades	15
Largest winning trade	$38,75.00	Largest losing trade	−$1,600.00
Average winning trade	$575.87	Average losing trade	−$597.75
Ratio avg. win/avg. loss	0.96	Avg. trade(win & loss)	$249.86
Max consec. winners	7	Max consec. losers	2
Avg. # bars in winners	2	Avg. # bars in losers	2
Max intraday drawdown	−$3,000.00		
Profit factor	2.50	Max # contracts held	1

Performance Summary: Short Trades

Total net profit	$37,471.25	Open position P/L	$0.00
Gross profit	$54,582.50	Gross loss	−$17,111.25
Total # of trades	64	Percent profitable	77%
Number winning trades	49	Number losing trades	15
Largest winning trade	$5,337.50	Largest losing trade	−$1,817.50
Average winning trade	$1,113.93	Average losing trade	−$1,140.75
Ratio avg. win/avg. loss	0.98	Avg. trade(win & loss)	$585.49
Max consec. winners	8	Max consec. losers	2
Avg. # bars in winners	2	Avg. # bars in losers	2
Max intraday drawdown	−$3,431.25		
Profit factor	3.19	Max # contracts held	1

Test Period	Trades	Net Profit	Avg. Trade	Profit Factor	Drawdown
1982-1988	56	$11,766	$210	1.90	($3,044)
1989-1997	62	$39,198	$632	4.02	($3,813)
1982-1987	49	$9,556	$195	1.85	($3,044)
1987-1992	37	$13,764	$372	4.80	($2,125)
1992-1997	39	$28,875	$740	3.57	($3,394)

RESULTS: Fake Out 01/04/82 − 12/31/97

PORTFOLIO PERSPECTIVE

After determining the signals for each market, the next step was to review the systems from a portfolio perspective. When combining signals and systems, there are several points to keep in mind. For example, if more than one rule is signaling a trade, which one should you follow? If you're currently in a trade and a new signal comes along, what should you do?

In assembling the portfolio, I assumed that if I were holding a position and a new signal came along in the same direction for the same market, I would ignore it. If I were holding a position and a new signal came along in the opposite direction, I would reverse my position. If I had multiple signals, I would take the one that would enter the market first. The simulated portfolio performance is shown below.

Performance Summary: All Trades			
Total net profit	$421,153.00	Open position P/L	$0.00
Total # of trades	1,079	Percent profitable	78%
Number winning trades	837	Number losing trades	242
Largest winning trade	$14,825.00	Largest losing trade	−$3,150.00
Average winning trade	$771.00	Average losing trade	−$925.00
Ratio avg. win/avg. loss	0.83	Avg. trade(win & loss)	$390.32
Max consec. winners	28	Max consec. losers	3
Max drawdown	−$10,375.00		
Profit factor	2.88	Max # contracts held	1

Year	Trades	Net Profit	Profit Factor	Drawdown
1997	77	$99,138	4.68	($8,688)
1996	78	$38,306	3.82	($3,925)
1995	71	$18,013	1.75	($4,944)
1994	64	$28,963	2.55	($10,375)
1993	64	$14,206	2.12	($5,856)
1992	61	$19,400	5.26	($2,706)
1991	57	$21,294	3.24	($4,050)
1990	71	$25,931	4.31	($2,100)
1989	79	$35,259	7.44	($3,306)
1988	67	$19,659	2.60	($3,553)
Average	69	$32,017	3.78	($4,950)

RESULTS: COMBINED PORTFOLIO
01/04/82 − 12/31/97

Although I didn't do this at the time, I now make it standard practice to do a more in-depth drawdown analysis. The summary shows a drawdown of $10,375. With a starting account value of only $14,000, that's a cause for concern. It's rare that real-time trading produces a lower drawdown. In fact, even in the simulation world, you can just put the hypothetical trades in a different order and get a drastically different result. In the extreme case all losing trades could occur consecutively resulting in a drawdown equal to the gross loss, but the probability of that happening is very small.

I used a Monte Carlo technique, which by definition takes into account the random order of trades and the resulting impact on a system's drawdown. As an example, consider the bond trading system below:

Total net profit	$28,350.00	Open position P/L	$0.00
Gross profit	$46,729.00	Gross Loss	$18,379.00
Total # of trades	66	Percent profitable	77%
Number winning trades	51	Number losing trades	15
Largest winning trade	$3,625.00	Largest losing trade	−$2,375.00
Average winning trade	$916.25	Average losing trade	−$1,225.27
Ratio avg. win/avg. loss	0.75	Avg. trade(win & loss)	$429.55
Max consec. winners	8	Max consec. losers	3
Max drawdown	−$4,799.00		
Profit factor	2.54	Max # contracts held	1

For these 66 trades in the order that they occurred, the drawdown was $4,799.00. If all the losing trades occurred consecutively, our drawdown would equal the gross loss of $18,379. And if the trades occurred in any other order, we'd most likely get a different drawdown yet. If we randomize the trade order 1,000 times and plot the drawdown distribution, we'd see plots similar to the ones shown below. The top graph represents the distribution of drawdowns observed. The bottom graph represents the cumulative probability curve of the drawdown distribution. As seen, the majority of simulated drawdowns were in the $4,000 area. Some occurrences as large as $12,000 were seen, but those happened much less often (if we ran a sufficiently large sample, we would eventually expect to see the max drawdown when all the losing trades occur consecutively). From the cumulative plot we see that the likelihood of exceeding a $4,000 drawdown is approximately 40%. Likewise, there is less than a 10% chance that we would expect to exceed a $6,000 drawdown. These data can be valuable in establishing account sizes and drawdown expectation.

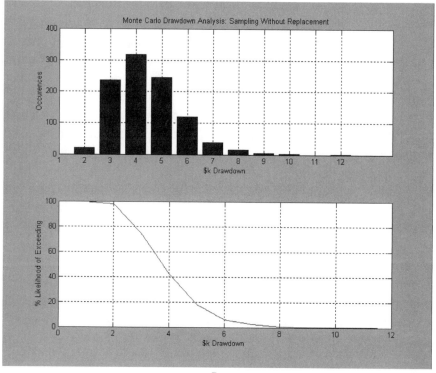

REPRINTED WITH PERMISSION OF THE MATHWORKS

Specifically, the trade order was randomized several times and the simulated drawdown from each trial was logged. From this, I could determine the likelihood that a certain drawdown value would be exceeded. In my present work, I try to keep the likelihood of exceeding my drawdown threshold at 10% or less. Or alternatively, I might take the 10% drawdown value and use that to help set the starting account size.

Money Management

With the signals now defined and a total portfolio view examined, the next step was to consider money management. This is an area that is often overlooked by new traders. Before I entered the World Cup competition, I started a trading account with $20,000. Eleven months and 98 trades later, I had managed to trade this account up to $66,612 on a single contract basis. But when I reviewed my trades in light of several money management techniques I had learned about, I was shocked to see what I *could* have accomplished: My $66,000 account could have turned into $421,568 — a more than eight-fold increase in profits!

Could I have realistically traded my account to this level? Probably not, but it was certainly a great example to demonstrate the power of money management. In my approach to the 1998 *World Cup Championship,* I was certainly committed to establishing a formal money management plan. I urge every trader to incorporate money management into their trading strategy in order to allocate capital efficiently to reduce risk and maximize profits.

The first approach I studied was optimal fraction (Optimal f), although I knew I would probably not implement it directly. That will become clear in a bit, but first an overview of the strategy. Optimal f aims to maximize profits from a series of trades, and was pioneered by Ralph Vince in his book *Portfolio Management Formulas.* For systems in which the size of the wins is constant and the size of the losses is constant, Optimal f can be calculated fairly easily using the payoff ratio (win/loss ratio) and the accuracy. In formula form, it looks like this: (Note that this is also known as the Kelly technique.)

$$fraction\ to\ wager = \frac{(Payoff\ Ratio + 1) * Accuracy - 1}{Payoff\ Ratio}$$

When the size of the wins and losses varies, such as in futures trading, calculating the Optimal f is a more mathematically involved endeavor. (The details can be found in Vince's book.) To summarize here, once we know the optimal fraction we arrive at the number of contracts to trade by taking our largest loss, dividing it by the optimal fraction and then dividing our account balance by this result. Optimal f can lead to spectacular returns, and it can be the fastest way to realize account growth. In the case of my model portfolio, in hypothetical testing the returns quickly reached millions of dollars.

Implementing Optimal f in real-time trading, however, is difficult if not impossible. First of all, calculating an Optimal f value requires a series of trades. So the question then becomes, do you use your hypothetical trades to calculate what fraction to start using in real-time trading? Or do you wait to get a set of real-time trades in order to validate your system's logic and then start employing Optimal f?

Lastly, highly accurate systems result in large optimal fractions. In many cases the Optimal f can exceed 50% or 60%. This means that in real-time trading the moment you realize your largest loss you see a drawdown of 50% or 60%. Most people, myself included, cannot handle that psychologically. In addition, for some systems the funds simply aren't available to support the total margin requirement.

As the chart below illustrates, given the margin limit, I could not use Optimal f to trade the markets I had chosen.

Market	Optimal Fraction	Margin Limit	Result
NYFE	66%	62%	Optimal f not possible. Margin limited.
Bonds	61%	73%	Optimal f possible. Not margin limited.
Coffee	70%	24%	Optimal f not possible. Margin limited.

A more practical approach was to devise a fixed fractional plan that would accommodate both drawdown and margin issues.

Here's the basis of my fixed fractional plan: Prior to each trade, I would take 40% of my account equity (not including open position profits) and divide that by the margin requirement to arrive at the number of contracts to use. If your stop-loss value is less than the margin requirement, you are not actually risking 40% of the account value. Instead, you are in effect allocating 40% of your capital to support the trade, making this money unavailable as margin for other transactions. I imagine it would be possible to achieve the same results by just using a lower fractional value and dividing by the maximum loss (or stop-loss), but I chose to set it up this way. Using this 40% rule, I simulated what the annual improvement over single-contract trading would have been on my portfolio, as the chart below illustrates.

Year	Net Profit	Drawdown	vs. Single Contract
1997	$1,321,181	$49,400	13.3x
1996	$329,638	$83,200	8.6x
1995	$9,819	$15,350	0.5x
1994	$32,863	$31,675	1.1x
1993	$38,800	$4,606	2.7x
1992	$44,656	$10,325	2.3x
1991	$73,119	$7,800	3.4x
1990	$52,513	$6,031	1.1x
1989	$73,574	$43,563	2.1x
1988	$21,799	$8,145	1.1x

Looking at these results, a couple of points become very clear. First, I wish would have done this exercise in 1996 and joined the contest in 1997! The money management improvement of 13.3x would have yielded a net profit over one million dollars — a return that even rivals Larry William's legendary account in 1987. That's the obvious one. A more subtle, yet revealing point is that in 1995 the 40% formula would have resulted in a *lower return* compared to single contract trading. This proves that there are no guarantees with any strategy or system.

The larger drawdowns are a direct consequence of increasing the number of contracts traded. In essence, this meant using the "bank's" money, which is not a cause for concern. Now let's see how all of this actually worked.

THE RESULTS

With the signal research complete and a money management plan in place, 1998 arrived and I was ready to test everything I had learned and accomplished thus far in the ultimate arena: the World Cup. As the summary of my 1998 World Cup performance shows, I had a total net profit of $13,290.95. My overall return was 95%, which was good enough for first place in the non-professional division and second place overall.

Total net profit	$13,290.95	Open position P/L	$0.00
Total # of trades	63	Percent profitable	65%
Number winning trades	41	Number losing trades	22
Largest winning trade	$5,111.45	Largest losing trade	–$3,237.60
Average winning trade	$1,112.56	Average losing trade	–$1,469.27
Ratio avg. win/avg. loss	0.76	Avg. trade(win & loss)	$210.97
Max consec. winners	7	Max consec. losers	3
Max drawdown	–$9,872.75		
Profit factor	1.41	Max # contracts held	2

ACTUAL 1998 WORLD CUP PERFORMANCE: ALL TRADES

While I am proud of what I accomplished, I cannot rest on my laurels. I continually learn not only from what I did well, but from my mistakes and misjudgments as well. By studying past performance — of my systems and of myself as a trader — I can see where to make improvements as new strategies and methodologies are developed and new market opportunities present themselves. The same commitment to improve that I had in the beginning continues today.

Thus, I went back and examined my 1998 performance, comparing what I did to what I *could* have done. Had I stuck to my systems exactly, I theoretically could have achieved about a 163% return. Incidentally, that would have been good enough for first place in the professional division that year as well.

In the following table, details of the simulated 1998 World Cup performance are presented. For this comparison, I reviewed my real-time trades and calculated the average slippage I incurred for each market. I deducted this as well as the commission rate I paid from each of the simulated trades.

Total net profit	$22,753.88	Open position P/L	$0.00
Total # of trades	66	Percent profitable	70%
Number winning trades	46	Number losing trades	20
Largest winning trade	$14,150.60	Largest losing trade	−$8,666.76
Average winning trade	$18,60.88	Average losing trade	−$3,142.34
Ratio avg. win/avg. loss	0.59	Avg. trade(win & loss)	$344.76
Max consec. winners	8	Max consec. losers	5
Max drawdown	−$20,255.70		
Profit factor	1.36	Max # contracts held	6

SIMULATED 1998 WORLD CUP PERFORMANCE:
ALL TRADES

A theoretical 163% versus an actual 95% return? What accounted for the difference in performance? Clearly, several factors were involved: misquotes referencing where the markets opened, missed orders on the floor, computer troubles just to name a few. The biggest reason is that trading is simply a tough business. It takes hard work and discipline. Following a trading plan exactly is also very difficult. The human element — fear, greed, doubt, second-guessing, relying on hunches — can get in the way of even the best designed and most thoroughly tested system. In fact, the first trade I made in my World Cup account was in live cattle! I devoted so much effort to formulate my trading rules, choose my markets and develop my system — and what did I trade? A totally unrelated market. At the time, I thought that live-cattle trade was a "sure thing." And, naturally, it was logged into the negative column.

> **What accounted for the difference in performance?... The biggest reason is that trading is simply a tough business. It takes hard work and discipline.**

Never underestimate the psychological aspect. Trading real money is an emotional experience. Just read some of my journal entries from the competition:

07-MAY	"Gambled here a bit and got stung..."
17-JUN	"Should I exit NYFE at close (against the rule)?"
22-JUL	"Rough day! Stopped out of NYFE at day's low only to see market turn..."
18-AUG	"Take a breather! No short term signals. Sit on the sidelines and relax!!"
13-SEP	"Decided to sit tight. Looks like a costly mistake."
14-SEP	"Blew this one! Got greedy?"
12-OCT	"Note: This was not by the book."
27-OCT	"Following rule exactly would have increased profit $2,500. Something to be said about following the rules!"
02-DEC	"...followed the rule exactly this time (and it hurt) but I've got to follow the rules exactly ALL the time."

The journal entries also show just how exciting and challenging futures trading can be. It's possible to achieve success, but not without a lot of hard work to develop a winning trading system and to have the discipline to follow it each and every trading day.

CHAPTER 4

SUCCESSFUL STOCK INDEX TRADING: USING A TIMING APPROACH FOR CONSISTENT RETURNS

BY CHUCK HUGHES

To determine the market's direction, whether an intra-day move or a short-term trend, the best strategy for the average trader is a mechanical trading system that eliminates emotional decision-making. A mechanical system allows you to play the game of percentages and probability, putting the odds in your favor by using a methodology that has a long history of success and does not rely on "guessing" future price movement.

As I learned in my early days of trading, emotional decision-making can be your worst enemy. However, a mechanical system can remove this emotional element from trading. A trading system eliminates "gut feelings," second guesses, whims, uninformed decision making, and a host of other emotional responses, which cause you to fail to obtain a consistent and reasonable rate of return. A simple trading system can help alleviate this problem.

In this chapter, I will discuss my methods for devising or adapting a trading system. The most important consideration is to make sure the trading system suits you. A system may be highly profitable and show great results, but if it exceeds your risk tolerance or if it does not match your trading style or even your personality, it will be of little use to you in the long run. By contrast, when you have a mechanical system that allows you to trade according to your own parameters, and you apply it to a highly liquid and efficient market, you have a winning combination.

For me, that means trading stock index futures, as I have experienced in my own trading and which led, ultimately, to my *World Cup*

Championship. The purpose of the stock index systems presented in this chapter is to not only to beat the historical long-term return generated by stocks, but also to do so with considerably less risk compared to a buy-and-hold strategy.

When it comes to trading systems, simple is better. The more complicated a system is, the less likely it will be successful in the future. I prefer those that have a long history of profitability in any type of market condition while incurring little risk. Of course, there is no guarantee that a system that has performed well in the past will continue to do so in the future. The best overall strategy, therefore, is to utilize several different types of mechanical systems with the hope that the majority will continue to perform well in the future.

TRADING WITH A SYSTEM

One of the biggest mistakes made by individuals is that they tend to let losses run and cut gains short. Researchers have concluded that this is due to a mental attitude called "loss aversion." The average trader finds that losses, even small losses, are very painful. Also, in their minds a loss is not real until the position or investment is actually sold and the loss is final. As long as they're still holding on, there is still a chance (no matter how slim) that the position could turn around and break even or generate a profit. At the same time, most people want to lock in gains and quickly realize them. No matter if the market keeps moving without them. They get great satisfaction from locking in a small gain.

One way to avoid these common mistakes is to utilize a mechanical trading system that dictates strict buy and sell rules. These rules are based on identifying patterns in the markets that have historically proven to be consistently profitable over long periods of time and under all types of market conditions.

Here are my top criteria for a good trading system:

EIGHT ESSENTIAL ELEMENTS FOR A GOOD TRADING SYSTEM

A good trading system:
- is totally mechanical
- does not give you any choices or decisions to make
- is not subjective or open to interpretation
- tells you exactly when and at what price trades should be entered and exited
- provides trading information with clear, concise and easy to understand rules
- has a long history of profitability in any type of market condition
- is low risk and provides consistent returns without the use of leverage
- takes only a few minutes to implement

With a good trading system, trading decisions are governed by a predetermined set of rules that have historically provided consistent, market-beating returns. With this understanding, here is a stock index system that utilizes seasonal analysis.

IDENTIFYING SEASONAL PATTERNS

One way of identifying seasonal patterns in stocks is to focus on the major stock indices such as the Dow Jones Industrial Average, S&P 500 Index, Nasdaq Composite, the Russell 2000 Index, etc. Daily prices are available for the Dow as far back as 1902, the S&P 500 back to 1928, and the Nasdaq Composite back to 1971.

Studying a year's worth of daily price bars for the Dow over each of the last 50 years, it would eventually become obvious that there are, indeed, seasonal tendencies in the price of stocks. Doing that, however, would also be very labor intensive. A much simpler way would be to use the power of the computer to assist with the study.

There are different ways of constructing seasonal charts. The most popular way is to construct a chart that shows how far prices extend from their statistical norm. The charts on the next few pages, however, were created using a completely different and much simpler approach. First, the highest price a market traded during a year was identified. The lowest price traded was subtracted from the highest price, which resulted in the annual price range. Next, by converting each day's closing price into a percentage of the annual range, a chart was constructed, based entirely on these percentages.

A percentage chart assigns each day a number between 0 and 100, representing where that day closed relative to the price range for the year. After converting the data for each year of the study, it can be blended together by simply adding the values and calculating an average. Chart 4.1 depicts the percentage changes in the Dow over a 25-year period from 1950 to 1974.

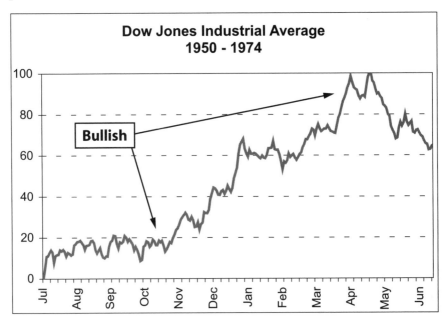

CHART 4.1   PERCENTAGE CHART FOR THE DOW
1950–1974

Note that on Chart 4.1, the period from November through April is very bullish and accounts for most of the gain in the Dow. This chart starts in July instead of January so as to better depict the bullish period. Viewing the Dow with a blended chart that connects December to January also makes it possible to see the bullish period much more clearly. Chart 4.2 is a blended chart that shows the second half of our study, covering the 25 years from 1975 through 1999.

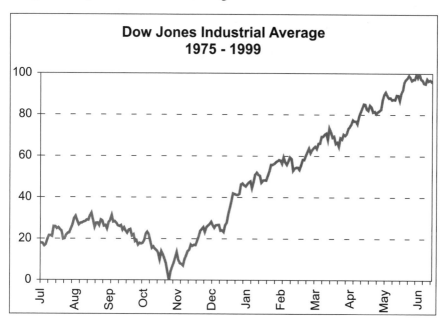

CHART 4.2   Percentage Chart for Dow 1975–1999

Chart 4.2 also shows a bullish period from November through April. Based on these two charts, a fair assessment would be that most of the gains in the Dow in the last 50 years have occurred during the six-month period from November through April. This bullish seasonal period was first discovered by Yale Hirsch, author of the *Stock Trader's Almanac*.

CONFIRMATION BY THE
S&P 500 AND NASDAQ

Can this bullish seasonal pattern from November through April be confirmed by a similar examination of the S&P 500 Index? The answer lies in the charts of the S&P 500 Index for these same 25-year periods. As might be expected, the seasonal patterns for the S&P 500, as seen in Charts 4.3 and 4.4, are very similar to those for the Dow.

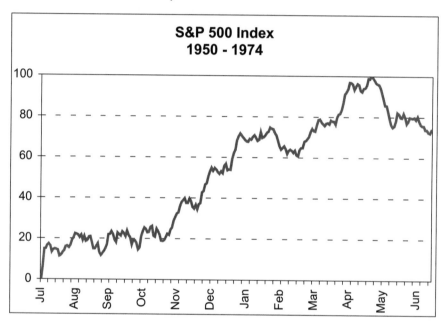

CHART 4.3   PERCENTAGE CHART FOR S&P 500 1950–1974

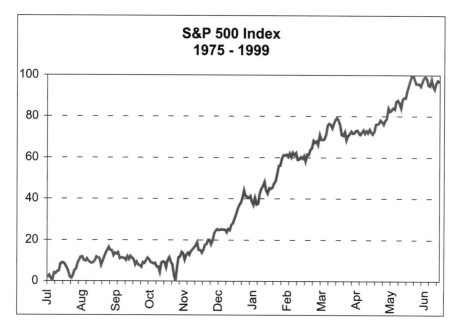

CHART 4.4   CHART CAPTION: PERCENTAGE CHART
FOR S&P 500 1975–1999

Looking at the data compiled for the Nasdaq Composite since 1971, patterns emerge. In Chart 4.5, the first 15 years of data are depicted. Although Chart 4.5 does appear to confirm the bottom in November, it does not confirm a top in April as seen in the Dow and S&P 500 charts. Instead, during this first 15-year period, the Nasdaq appears to have continued a bullish tendency through June.

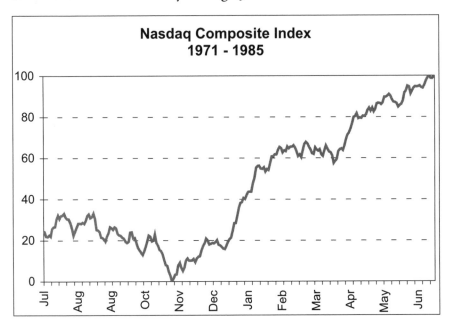

CHART 4.5   CHART CAPTION: PERCENTAGE CHART FOR NASDAQ 1971–1985

Chart 4.6, depicting the second 15-year period from 1986 through 2000, once again confirms the tendency for the market to bottom in November and continue its bullish bias through June. Overall, it appears from this analysis of blended percentage charts that the most favorable time to be invested in S&P 500 and Dow stocks is during the six-month period from the November through April. The best time to own Nasdaq stocks is from November through June.

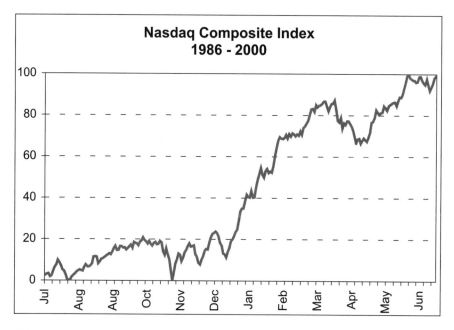

CHART 4.6   PERCENTAGE CHART FOR NASDAQ 1986–2000

To get the full impact of the results of the study, the next step would be to take a look at how various investment portfolios might have performed during the last 52 years for the S&P 500 and during the last 31 years for the Nasdaq Composite.

A Buy-and-Hold Approach

To test the seasonal analysis, assume that $10,000 was invested in the S&P 500 Index in 1950. As of September 2002, the value of the portfolio would be $507,741.74. Chart 4.7 shows the growth of the investment over time.

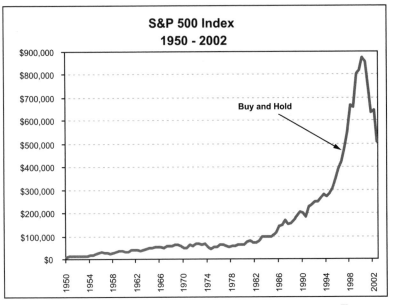

CHART 4.7   S&P Index Buy and Hold Results 1950–2002

A BASIC TIMING APPROACH

Now it's time to take a different approach, based on the seasonal study. This time, assume that the S&P 500 index was purchased on November 1st each year and sold on April 30th of the following year, instead of being invested at all times. During the six months that no position was held in the market, all funds were invested in five-year Treasury Notes or similar short-term fixed income securities.

Using this basic timing approach, the hypothetical $10,000 investment in 1950 grew to $1,526,256.29 as of September 2002. This translates to a *200% increase in return when compared to the buy-and-hold approach with only half of the risk!* As Chart 4.8 shows, the timing approach produced a better return with less risk.

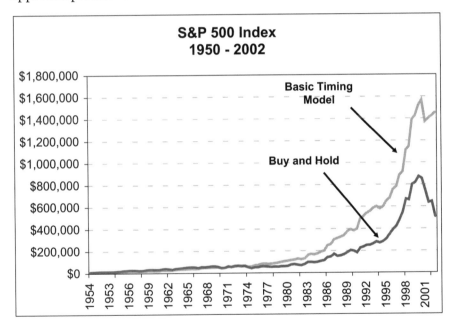

CHART 4.8   TIMING THE MARKET VS. BUY AND HOLD

This basic timing approach using the S&P 500 Index would have resulted in profits in 45 of the last 53 years or 84.9% winning years. On only three occasions would the yearly loss have been greater than 10% with the largest losing year producing a 13.5% loss.

THE NASDAQ

Now, compare the basic timing system versus a buy-and-hold approach in the Nasdaq Composite. Chart 4.9 shows the growth of $10,000 invested in the Nasdaq in 1971 using a buy-and-hold approach. As of September 2002, the value of such a portfolio would have been $111,187.97.

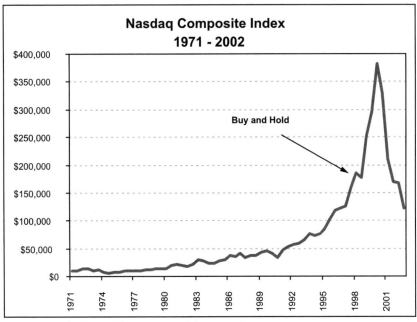

CHART 4.9   BUY-AND-HOLD APPROACH IN THE NASDAQ COMPOSITE

By comparison, Chart 4.10 shows the growth of $10,000 invested in the Nasdaq Composite in 1971 using the basic timing system. The index was purchased on November 1st and sold on April 30th. During the six months that no position was held in the market, all funds were invested in 5-year Treasury Notes. Using this basic timing system, the $10,000 investment in 1971 grew to $427,631.26 as of September 2002. This translates to a 284% increase in return compared to the buy-and-hold approach with only half of the risk. This proves once again that timing the market produces a better return with less risk.

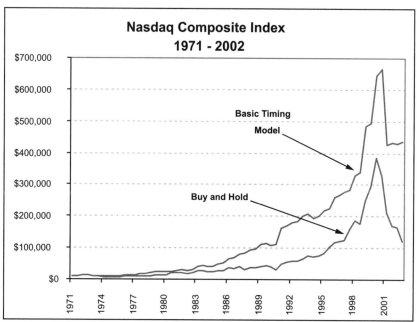

CHART 4.10   TIMING THE MARKET VS. BUY AND HOLD IN NASDAQ

This basic timing system is simple: It does not require a computer, nor a great deal of time or energy. Furthermore, over the last 52 years, it has proven to be more profitable than a buy-and-hold approach with only half the risk. But is it possible to further improve upon this risk-adjusted return? Take a closer look at seasonal patterns that produce market-beating returns while at the same time reducing risk even further than the November through April seasonal timing system just presented.

The Nasdaq — A Closer Look

Much has been said about the tendency of the tech stocks to rally during the December–January time period. With the help of 31 years of daily price data, it's easy to see December and January are indeed the best months to own Nasdaq stocks.

Table 4.1 shows the results of investing $10,000 in the Nasdaq Composite on December 1st and selling on January 31st each year since the inception of the index in 1971. Five-year Treasury Notes were purchased during the 10 months that funds were not invested in the Nasdaq Index. The total profit of $392,374 handily beat the $111,188 profit realized from a long-term buy-and-hold approach of being continuously invested in the index since 1971.

Total Profit $	$392,374
Percent Return	3,924%
Average Annual Return	131%
Percent Winning Years	96.8%
Total Number of Trades	31
# of Winning Trades	30
Percent Winning Trades	96.8%
Largest Loss	–2.8%
Total Profits	$411,154
Total Losses	($14,810)
Profit Factor	27.8
Based on investing $10,000 in Nasdaq Composite during December–January since 1971 (before commissions)	

Table 4.1

Nasdaq Timing System (Dec–Jan) Historical Results 1971–2001

Not only does this timing system produce a superior return, it also does so with considerably less risk. Following this system, funds are invested in the index *17% of the total trading days* each year and held in Treasury securities during the balance of the other 83% of trading days.

This timing strategy incurred some small losses with the purchase and sale of the Nasdaq Index, but the interest earned from the 5-year Treasury Notes for the most part offset the losses from the index trades. As Table 4.1 shows, only one small net losing trade of −2.8% resulted over the past 31 years for this strategy. More than 96% of trades were profitable.

During the recent 2000–2001 bear market, the Nasdaq Composite lost over 70% of its value. This simple timing system produced a 32.6% *profit* during the same bear market. As Chart 4.11 shows as well as detailed in the trade-by-trade results that follow (see Appendix, end of chapter), the system also made a 10.6% profit during the severe 1973–1974 bear market when the index lost 66% of its value. The profit factor is 27.8 with over $27 of profit for each $1 of loss. Keep in mind that these results were achieved without the use of leverage or margin. The use of Nasdaq futures contracts would increase the profits and losses depending on the amount of margin used.

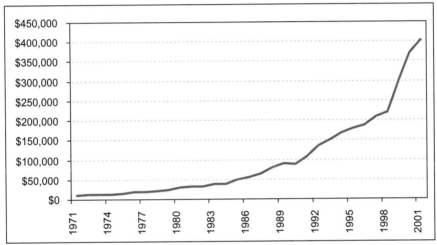

CHART 4.11   NASDAQ TIMING SYSTEM
(DECEMBER/JANUARY PROFIT GRAPH)

EXCHANGE TRADED FUNDS

In recent years, instruments have been introduced which can be bought or sold like a stock or similar security. By buying and selling these Exchange Traded Funds (ETFs), investors can enter or exit a position in an index, or establish a long or short position. The S&P 500 Index can be traded using ETFs such as *iShares, Webs, SPDRs, or HOLDRs.* The most popular ETF for the S&P 500 Index is the SPDRs (known as "spiders").

Spiders are traded much like stocks. Purchasing these instruments will yield the same return as the S&P 500, including dividends paid on individual stocks in the index.

Similar products are available for the Dow and the Nasdaq 100. The ETF for the Dow is referred to as "diamonds" (symbol DIA). The ETF for the Nasdaq 100 is known as "queens" or by their symbol "QQQ." There are also a wide variety of mutual funds available that track the major stock indexes such as the S&P 500, Nasdaq 100, Dow, and Russell 2000 Index to name a few. Note that there are no ETFs that track the Nasdaq Composite. There are ETF tracking securities such as the QQQs and Nasdaq 100 Index mutual funds that track the Nasdaq 100 Index, which is a close proxy for the Nasdaq Composite.

Using the ETF (symbol QQQ), here are the rules for the Nasdaq Timing System:

Nasdaq Timing System Rules

1. **Buy the Nasdaq 100 Index ETF (QQQ) on December 1st. (Nasdaq 100 Index Mutual Funds should be purchased on the close of November 30th.)**

2. **Sell the Nasdaq 100 QQQs or index mutual funds on January 31st.**

3. **Purchase 5-year Treasury Notes (or similar short term fixed income investment) with the proceeds and hold until December 1st when the QQQs will be purchased again.**

Small Cap Stocks

Investors may be familiar with the so-called "January effect" rally in small cap stocks that normally occurs in January each year. Historical price data reveals that January is indeed a good time to own small cap stocks. Over the last 52 years, $10,000 invested in small cap stocks during the month of January (and investing in 5-Year Treasury Notes for the remainder of the year) would have grown to a staggering $2,683,174. Table 4.2 shows historical results.

Total Profit $	$2,673,174
Percent Return	26,732%
Average Annual Return	514%
Percent Winning Years	98.0%
Total Number of Trades	52
# of Winning Trades	51
Percent Winning Trades	98.0%
Largest Loss	−.71%
Total Profits	$2,765,471
Total Losses	($2,296)
Profit Factor	29.9

Based on investing $10,000 in small cap stocks in January since 1950 (before commissions)

TABLE 4.2
SMALL CAP TIMING SYSTEM
HISTORICAL RESULTS
1950–2001

NOTE: Small cap stocks are defined as a portfolio of stocks represented by the fifth capitalization quintile (bottom 20%) of stocks on the New York Stock Exchange from 1926–1981. Small cap stocks are then defined by the performance of the Dimensional Fund Advisors (DFA) Small Company Fund from 1982 through March 2001, and then the performance of the DFA Micro Cap Fund from April 2001 to present. Capitalization represents the size of a company, calculated by multiplying the number of shares outstanding by the current price of a stock.

Capitalizing on the January effect results in a timing system that has historically generated market-beating results with comparatively less risk. This system is invested in stock for only one month a year resulting in only an 8% market exposure, and invested in secure Treasury securities during the balance of the other 92% of trading days. There was only one small loss of less than 1% during the 52-year period depicted in Chart 4.12. Results show that 98% of all trades were profitable and the profit factor was a healthy 29.9 with more than $29 of profit for each $1 of loss. (See trade-by-trade profit table in the Appendix of this chapter). Again, these results were achieved without the use of leverage or margin. The use of Russell 2000 futures contracts would increase the profits and losses depending on the amount of margin used.

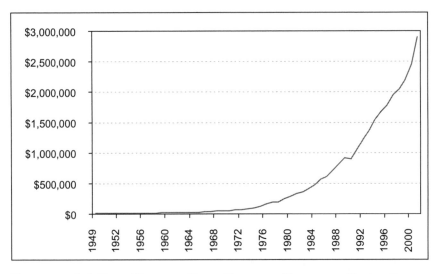

CHART 4.12   SMALL CAP TIMING SYSTEM PROFIT
GRAPH

SMALL CAP TIMING SYSTEM RULES

1. **Buy the Dimensional Fund Advisors Micro Cap Mutual Fund (symbol DFSCX) on the last trading day in December. (Mutual funds cannot be purchased on the open on the first trading day in January.)**

2. **Sell the DFSCX mutual fund on the last trading day in January.**

3. **Purchase 5-year Treasury Notes (or similar short term fixed income investment) with the proceeds and hold until the last trading day of December when the DFSCX mutual fund will be purchased again.**

CYCLE ANALYSIS

While the discussion thus far has focused on seasonal trading, a system can be based on any number of market indicators and recurring signals. In the next analysis, the system is based on market cycles — bullish or bearish moves that recur over regular time intervals. The focus of this system is on short-term cycles that recur monthly.

One of the most consistent bullish cycles in the stock market is the tendency of the market to rally during the last few trading days of the month and first few trading days of the new month. (This bullish tendency was first discovered by Yale Hirsch, author of the *Stock Trader's Almanac*.)

Daily price data demonstrates that this monthly cycle has been very consistent over the past 53 years, as evidenced by the trading results that follow. This bullish cycle is probably due to the tendency of institutions to purchase stocks at the end of the month — sometimes called "window dressing" — and the investment of employee payroll deductions for retirement accounts during the first few days of the new month.

This cycle system buys the S&P 500 Index on the second to last trading day of the month and exits on the third trading day of the new month, resulting in a five-day trade. Research with daily price data reveals that investing during this cycle not only delivers superior returns compared to a "buy-and-hold" approach, but also does so with considerably less risk. The system is only invested 17% of the total trading days and is invested in secure 5-year Treasury Notes during the balance of the other 83% of trading days.

The 53-year trading results in Table 4.3 and depicted in Chart 4.13 reveal that 75% of the 472 cycle system trades were profitable, producing a $4,096,108 profit. These strong, market-beating results were achieved with only a 17% market exposure, and 94% of yearly results were profitable. The largest losing trade was a −4.6%. Keep in mind that 10 bear markets occurred during this period, resulting in an average loss of 30.5% in the S&P 500 Index. As in the previous examples, these results were achieved without the use of leverage or margin. The use of S&P 500 futures contracts would increase the profits and losses depending on the amount of margin used.

Total Profit	$4,096,108
Percent Return	40,961%
Average Annual Return	772%
Percent Winning Years	94.3%
Total Number of Trades	472
# Winning Trades	354
Percent Winning Trades	75.0%
Largest Losing Trade	–4.6%
Total Profits	$5,109,897
Total Losses	($1,013,789)
Profit Factor	5.0

Based on investing $10,000 in the S&P 500 Cycle System in 1949–2001 (before commissions).

TABLE 4.3

S&P 500 CYCLE SYSTEM HISTORICAL RESULTS 1949 — 2001

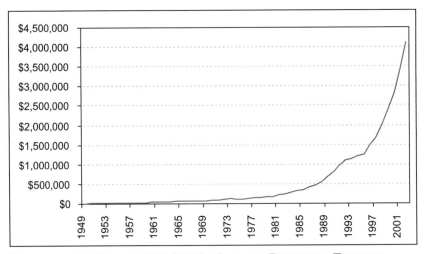

CHART 4.13   S&P 500 CYCLE SYSTEM PROFIT GRAPH

As Chart 4.14 illustrates, during most of the years that the S&P 500 Index had a negative return, the S&P 500 cycle system produced a positive return. Notice that during the 1973–1974 bear market the S&P 500 Index lost 47.1% but the S&P 500 cycle system only lost 6.5%.

During 2000–2001 the S&P 500 Index lost 23.2% but the monthly cycle system produced a 39.4% *profit*.

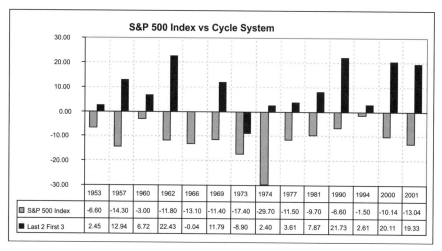

	1953	1957	1960	1962	1966	1969	1973	1974	1977	1981	1990	1994	2000	2001
☐ S&P 500 Index	-6.60	-14.30	-3.00	-11.80	-13.10	-11.40	-17.40	-29.70	-11.50	-9.70	-6.60	-1.50	-10.14	-13.04
■ Last 2 First 3	2.45	12.94	6.72	22.43	-0.04	11.79	-8.90	2.40	3.61	7.87	21.73	2.61	20.11	19.33

CHART 4.14   CYCLE SYSTEM RESULTS DURING DOWN YEARS IN THE S&P 500 INDEX

The S&P 500 cycle system performs better when there has not been a substantial rally in the index prior to entering a trade. A simple rule comparing today's S&P 500 Index closing price to the index price five trading days prior can be used to filter out trades after a substantial price increase in the index.

S&P 500 CYCLE SYSTEM RULES

1. **Buy the S&P 500 Index ETF (symbol SPY) on the market open on the second to last trading day of the month. S&P 500 Index mutual funds can be purchased on the third to last trading day of the month as mutual funds normally cannot be purchased on the market open on the second to last trading day of the month.**

2. **Sell the S&P 500 Index ETF or mutual funds on the close of the third trading day of the new month.**

3. **Purchase 5-year Treasury Notes (or similar short-term fixed income investment) with the proceeds and hold until the second to last trading day of the month when the index will be purchased again.**

4. **Do not take a trade if on the close of the third to last trading day of the month the S&P 500 Index has rallied more than 2 % since the index close five trading days prior. Also, do not enter trades in the summer months of July and August, which historically have not been good periods to trade and have not been profitable.**

5. **When the index is purchased, place a protective stop order to sell the index if the price drops 5% or more below the purchase price.**

PUTTING SYSTEMS TO WORK

The stock index systems presented in this chapter produce steady, market-beating returns during all types of market conditions. Remember that there were 10 bear markets throughout this testing period during which an average decline of 30.5% was experienced in the S&P 500 Index. These bear markets included the 1973–1974 decline in which the S&P 500 Index lost 48% of its value and the 2000–2002 decline in which the index lost 50% of its value.

These systems were designed to be simple in nature with just a few rules that are easily implemented by even the most inexperienced trader. With a little discipline, these systems are a powerful, low risk way to trade the stock indexes.

More importantly, these results show the power of using a system to trade rather than relying on your own judgment, which can become clouded by fear, doubt, greed, and second-guessing. Most successful traders — including the vast majority of World Cup winners — use systems that incorporate the trading rules and methodology that have been analyzed and proven through back testing. While the past is no guarantee of tomorrow's performance, using systems that have produced consistent returns over the years is a far better way of trading profitably today and into the future.

CHAPTER 5

SEASONAL TRADING SYSTEM

BY KURT SAKAEDA

Two of my great passions in life are gambling and trading. In fact, like myself, many of the most prominent traders (including *most* of the market players profiled in Jack Schwager's famous "Market Wizards" books) were, at one time, ardent gamblers who applied the skills they developed at the gaming tables to help them succeed at trading. Calculating probability statistics for counting cards, and assessing the risk potential of any gambling move, are tools that have enhanced my trading decisions and methods enormously. A great example of this merger of methods is my Seasonal Trading System, which propelled me to victory in the 2002 *World Cup Championship of Futures Trading,* and which I still use to this very day.

The seed for my method was planted over drinks one day with a friend who was a floor trader at the Chicago Mercantile Exchange. My friend suggested that it was possible to exploit opportunities in the commodities markets by identifying seasonal patterns. I thought it highly improbable, but I was intrigued by the possibilities. Always eager to find an edge that can increase my trading odds, I took his arguments to heart. I began crunching the numbers, and it soon became a decision that changed my life.

The deeper I delved into seasonal analysis, the more apparent it became that I was onto something potentially very lucrative. My objective was to develop a long-term approach to the markets based on patterns of price disparities that tend to occur on a seasonal basis. Simply put, I was looking to identify high and low price levels that occur on or near the same date year after year. After eight solid months of research and analysis, I had developed a seasonal model that has been providing solid results for me ever since. As you will see, the concept is simple, the calculations are straightforward and the resulting opportunities are outstanding.

THE FOUNDATIONS OF MY SEASON TRADING STRATEGY

To fully understand and employ my method, you must have a rudimentary knowledge of statistical analysis. I learned about statistics both in the classroom *and* at the tables at Caesar's Palace and The Flamingo. But don't let this put you off. With today's high-speed computers and the wide range of software support products available, anyone can easily assemble the data needed to apply my method and make it work.

To start, I calculate the average settlement price of a given commodity contract for each calendar day of the year, and then compare it against every other day of the year. Then I take the pick of the litter — the pair of dates with the largest price difference — and identify that as a potential trade. This produces trade initiations on both the long and short side of the market. My data tells me how much I can expect to profit, and how much I am reasonably risking by pursuing a similar move in the current year. Let's start with a brief introduction to the statistical tools I use on a regular basis.

> **AVERAGE:** The terms *average, mean,* and *expected value* are interchangeable. To find the average of a group of numbers, simply add together all the numbers in a data set and divide by the number of elements in the set.

For example, let's say we're looking for the average of a set of soybean prices. Assume there are five prices in the set: 510, 510 ¼, 510 ½, 511 and 514.

510
510 ¼
510 ½
511
514

510 = 510.00
510 ¼ = 510.25
510 ½ = 510.50
511 = 511.00
514 = 514.00

First convert fractions to decimals (510 ¼ = 510.25) and then add together all prices in the set.

510.00
510.25
510.50
511.00
514.00

2,555.75

The sum of these numbers is 2,555.75.

To determine the average, we would divide the sum by five, the number of elements in the set.

$$2,555.75 \div 5 = 511.15$$

That leaves us with an average price of 511.15. You'll notice that the average does not necessarily represent a tradable price; this average would fall between the futures pricing increments of 511 and 511 ¼. Nonetheless, it is important for us to determine the exact average for our analysis. My seasonal method requires determining a commodity contract's average price for each calendar day of the year, with the exception of the days immediately following contract expiration.

MEDIAN: The median value in a set of numbers is the midpoint, or the "guy in the middle." Median value tells about the distribution of numbers in a dataset.

It is easier to conceptualize median by putting the dataset in order of value. Let's say we are examining average settlement prices of March soybeans on February 12th each year from 1995 to 1999.

> ### Prices February 12
> **1995: 555 ¾**
> **1996: 717 ¾**
> **1997: 764 ¼**
> **1998: 682 ½**
> **1999: 492 ¼**

As happens typically, the numbers fall in random order: 555 ¾ in '95, 717 ¾ in '96, 764 ¼ in '97, 682 ½ in '98, and 492 ¼ in '99. However, we're looking for the midpoint. If we organize the numbers in order of value (492 ½, 555 ¾, 682 ½, 717 ¾, 764 ¼), it's easy to see that 682 ½ is our midpoint or median.

> ### Prices February 12
> 492 ¼
> 555 ¾
> **682 ½**
> 717 ¾
> 764 ¼

Had there been six items in our dataset instead of five, we would have taken the third and fourth element (now the *two* guys in the middle) and calculated their average.

> ### Prices February 12
> 492 ¼
> 505
> **555 ¾**
> **682 ½**
> 717 ¾
> 764 ¼

$$555 \tfrac{3}{4}$$
$$682 \tfrac{1}{2}$$
$$\overline{1{,}238 \tfrac{1}{4}}$$

$$1{,}238 \tfrac{1}{4} \div 2 = 618 \tfrac{3}{4}$$

492 ¼
505
555 ¾
618 ¾
682 ½
717 ¾
764 ¼

In all cases, we need to have an equal number of elements above and below the median element or elements. It is important to note that the median usually produces a number different from the average. The median helps reveal uneven distributions in a data set.

Here's an analogy to help you understand the concept of median. Some of you are parents sending your children to expensive colleges and universities. Suppose Big State University published statistics showing that graduating students last year secured jobs with an average starting salary of more than $70,000. It might seem that this is an attractive and useful figure until we analyze the data. We find that the total number of students in the graduating class is relatively small, with the vast majority actually taking jobs serving coffee at Starbucks. So what factor accounts for the high average starting salary? Closer inspection reveals that of the 100 BSU grads, one became CEO of the family business empire and earned $5.3 million. Most of the others earned around $18,000 serving mocha latte. In this example, we have an average of $70,820 *but a median of $18,000.* A significant difference between median and average in the same data set indicates that one or more extreme values are skewing the results.

$18,000 $18,000 $18,000 $18,000 $18,000 $18,000 $18,000 $18,000 $18,000
$18,000 $18,000 $18,000 $18,000 $18,000 $18,000 $18,000 $18,000 $18,000
$18,000 $18,000 $18,000 $18,000 $18,000 $18,000 $18,000 $18,000 $18,000
$18,000 $18,000 $18,000 $18,000 $18,000 $18,000 $18,000 $18,000 $18,000
$18,000 $18,000 $18,000 $18,000 $18,000 $18,000 $18,000 $18,000 $18,000
$18,000 $18,000 $18,000 $18,000 $18,000 $18,000 $18,000 $18,000 $18,000
$18,000 $18,000 $18,000 $18,000 $18,000 $18,000 $18,000 $18,000 $18,000
$18,000 $18,000 $18,000 $18,000 $18,000 **$5,300,000** $18,000 $18,000 $18,000
$18,000 $18,000 $18,000 $18,000 $18,000 $18,000 $18,000 $18,000 $18,000
$18,000 $18,000 $18,000 $18,000 $18,000 $18,000 $18,000 $18,000 $18,000
$18,000 $18,000 $18,000 $18,000 $18,000 $18,000 $18,000 $18,000 $18,000
$18,000

Average = $70,820
Median = $18,000

Let's look at another example of the difference between average and median. Every once in a while, state lotteries develop what is called a positive expectation. This happens when no one hits the jackpot for several drawings and the money in the prize pool rolls over several times. This may increase the worth of the average lottery ticket from its purchase price of $1.00 to perhaps $1.05 or $1.10. Does this mean this is the time to mortgage your house to buy lottery tickets? The answer is emphatically no! Even with hundreds of millions of lottery tickets, on average worth more than the purchase price, there will still be only a very limited number of winners. The median result will be a loss of one dollar. In this example, we have a negative median and a positive average, resulting in a fundamentally weak investment. (In one well-publicized instance, an Australian gambling syndicate formed a huge pool to purchase all possible combinations of numbers in one state lottery. After this notable "score," several states put in place impediments to prevent such practices.)

When a single anomaly drives the average out of whack, we have to consider the probability of the extreme value occurring again. In the context of the numbers we will be evaluating, a negative median profit means that the trade can be expected to be profitable less than 50% of the time, as an equal number of results must reside on both sides of the median. However, when a trade with a negative median pays off, it will pay off very well. Personally, I have an aversion to a trade set-up that is driven by one extraordinarily successful result. Although attractive averages generated by extreme values can translate to trades with large profits, the exceptional result we're looking for may not occur again for several years. The higher the median, the more consistent the result we can expect.

A positive median profit implies that we can expect a profitable trade more than 50% of the time. If the median profit is *significantly greater* than the average profit, we can expect a high percentage of profitable outcomes — but every once in a while we'll get a pronounced failure. For traders new to seasonal trading, I recommend passing on any trade carrying a negative median.

The optimal trade scenario occurs when the average gain and the median gain are equal. This indicates that the average is a meaningful "true average" and is not driven by extreme values. This forecasts a low probability for an extreme result to occur on either end of the spectrum.

STANDARD DEVIATION: Trading risk can be measured in units of standard deviation. I calculate risk to one unit of standard deviation, which translates to the amount that an outcome may be expected to deviate from the average profit approximately 68% of the time. Standard deviation is derived from a complex calculation using the squares of the distances from the average result to each actual result. The resultant number tells what to expect on the extremes. As standard deviation goes up, trades get riskier. This is critical in calculating potential losses.

One unit of standard deviation from the average profit is the number I add to both projected profit and loss to determine the extremes that might be encountered slightly more than two-thirds of the time. The second standard deviation unit encompasses approximately 68% of the remaining outcomes or about 95% of all outcomes. The third standard deviation unit encompasses approximately 68% of the remaining 5% of outcomes or about 99% of all outcomes. The larger the unit of standard deviation, the less likely a result outside the projected range is bound to occur.

Although we can never get to an absolute assurance of our potential extremes in trading, we can accurately define the probabilities. The following is a rough outline of how to read them:

- **When the elements of a data set are pretty tightly grouped together forming a steep bell-shaped curve, the standard deviation is small.**
- **When the elements are widely distributed forming a flatter bell curve, the standard deviation is larger.**
- **To entice us to enter into a position, the standard deviation of a potential trade must be in proportion to the amount we expect to gain; if we are looking at a modest average profit of $500 and a large standard deviation of $10,000, the expected profit does not justify to exposure to extreme loss.**
- **Ideally, we are looking for a high average price, a positive median profit, and a relatively low standard deviation. Typically, I find one standard deviation of up to five times the average profit to be in an acceptable range. I suggest bypassing trades carrying a standard deviation of five or more times the size of the average profit.**

Average profit = $1,000
Standard Deviation = $2,500

Outcomes within one standard deviation:
Profit up to $3,500
Loss up to $1,500

A trade with a $1,000 average profit may typically carry a standard deviation — the potential profit or loss beyond the average — of $2,500. This means that in slightly more than two-thirds of all cases, it can be expected that the result of entering that trade will fall between a profit of $3,500 and a loss of $1,500.

Average profit = $10,000
Standard Deviation = $20,000

Outcomes within one standard deviation:
Profit up to $30,000
Loss up to $10,000

If another trade carries an average gain of $10,000 but a standard deviation of $20,000, the potential exists for a gain of $30,000 or a loss of $10,000 in approximately 68% of all outcomes. This means that in approximately 32% of all outcomes, the gain or loss could exceed our projections.

MY SEASONAL METHOD

My model calculates an average price for every day of the year in a given commodity contract (i.e. March corn or May silver), minus the days immediately following contract expiration. This average price is determined using daily settlement prices going back as many years as available from the data vendor I use. (I purchase Bridge CRB data, but there are several reliable vendors to choose from.) Because any annual date (say May 28) will fall on a weekend and possibly a holiday as we move across many years, I assign weekend and holiday prices based on the interpolation (estimated value between two known values) of prices on the trading days surrounding the weekend or holiday. It is simply our best guess at what would have transpired on those days based on surrounding values. This smoothes out the rough edges in my calculations.

I also have to make allowance for the fact that some years do not produce a full 365 days of data. In its first year of trading, a contract may be launched on, say, May 15. In other instances, trading may have been suspended for prolonged periods of time due to exceptional circumstances; the 1996 copper trading scandal due to rouge trading of Sumitomo Corporation's Yasuo Hamanaka comes to mind.

Furthermore, I do not analyze data for the period of days extending from expiration day to the end of that month. This data is not relevant to my method, as my studies suggest a maximum "hold time" of 11 months.

Why use the settlement price as an indicator? Actually, tracking the average price in the opening range would work just as well. I use settlement prices because they are represented by a single price and are readily available.

Once I have the average settlement price for each day of the year, I calculate the price difference between every possible pair of days. This comprehensive analysis of 132,860 combinations (365 x 364) takes only about two minutes on my computer for each commodity contract. Then I calculate average profit, median profit, and standard deviation for the trade represented by the absolute high and low. As I currently track approximately 280 contracts, the run time for this analysis in MySQL using AWK language is approximately nine hours. There are several commercially available programs that can be used to generate these studies; I use MySQL because it is convenient and free. The download is free, but you may have to purchase support and training to learn how to run these studies.

Alternatively, you could simply scan for the highest and the lowest average settlement price to determine the single trade with the greatest potential for each particular contract. I prefer the prior method, as this provides secondary and tertiary trade opportunities within each contract, but for the most part I also rely heavily on identifying the highest high and the lowest low.

There are, however, occasional instances in which the high and low do not represent the best trading opportunity. This occurs when a comparable high or low can be identified closer to the anticipated exit date. A good example of this occurs in my data for January natural gas:

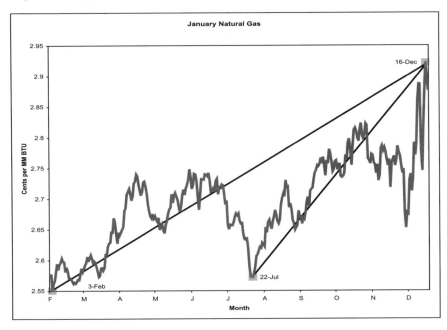

CHART 5.1   JANUARY NATURAL GAS

As you see on this chart, the vertical column represents price (in this case $2.55 to $2.95 per MM BTU) and the horizontal line represents the calendar days of the year. The chart tracks the average settlement price on each calendar day included for all months of available data. In this case, we are examining 12 months of data through 2002.

(As I do not enter into positions on the days immediately following contract expiration, my charts cover approximately 350 days of the year. For example, soybean meal contracts expire on the business day prior to the 15th of the month. Consequently, my July soybean meal chart will not include data for July 15–31.)

In January natural gas, the annual composite low occurs on February 3, and the annual composite high occurs on December 16. However, we can make a faster and safer trade by looking to enter long at a nearly comparable low price on July 22. We may not achieve quite as low of an entry price, but we will theoretically need to hold this trade less than half as long. That frees up margin money for other trades in the interim, and reduces the risk of outside events adversely affecting the normal seasonal trend. In this scenario, I'd rather face the prospect of making a projected profit of $3,498 over five months than $3,714 over 11 months.

A second important product of my research is the generation of price charts for each of the commodity contracts I currently track. I update these each January when new annual settlement data becomes available, and I keep them in a notebook I refer to as my Blue Book. You can easily develop a folder of charts yourself. All you need is a list of the contracts (commodity and delivery month) you want to profile, the historical settlement data, and some basic programming skills.

Symbol	Category	Exp. Month	Yrs. Data	Avg. Profit	Mdn. Profit	Std. Dev.
CT	Softs	December	43	834.26	290.00	4054.62
CD	Currencies	December	31	905.48	1000.00	3574.70
JO	Softs	November	36	681.25	772.50	2647.21
SI	Metals	May	39	4279.36	285.00	9098.09
SM	Grains	May	43	632.56	270.00	2152.74
HU	Energies	January	17	2900.72	1629.60	6202.32
NQ	Indicies	September	7	26233.57	15600.00	22923.37
HO	Energies	February	24	2498.48	1100.40	6262.43
LH	Livestock	February	36	1216.56	1520.00	3193.21
NP	Currency	March	7	5883.93	7650.00	4068.80

A SNAPSHOT OF BLUE BOOK TRADE SET-UPS WITH DATA INCLUSIVE THROUGH 2002.

Once I establish an entry and exit date for each contract, it becomes a simple matter of waiting for the entry date to arrive. I give myself two consecutive days of opportunity to enter each trade, starting with the actual entry date. If the entry date falls on a Saturday, I try to enter the market on the preceding Friday and the following Monday. If the entry date falls on a Sunday, I try to enter the market on the following Monday and Tuesday. If the entry date falls on a weekday holiday, I try to enter the market on the day preceding and the day after the holiday.

BUY CHECKLIST	
Current price must be at or below average settlement price for that date.	✔
Median profit must be a positive number.	✔
Standard deviation must be less than 5 times the average profit.	✔
The contract must not be trading at or near historical highs.	✔

If I am scheduled to buy long, I will enter an order to buy shortly after the opening of the market provided that 1) I can buy at or below the average settlement price indicated for that date*; 2) the median profit is a positive number; 3) the standard deviation is less than five times the average profit; and 4) the contract is not trading at or near historical highs.

SELL CHECKLIST	
Current price must be at or above average settlement price for that date.	✔
Median profit must be a positive number.	✔
Standard deviation must be less than 5 times the average profit.	✔
The contract must be not trading at or near historical lows.	✔

Conversely, if I am scheduled to sell short, I will enter an order to sell shortly after the opening provided that 1) I can sell at or above the average settlement price indicated for that date*; 2) the median profit is a positive number; 3) the standard deviation is less than five times the average profit; and 4) the contract is not trading at or near historical lows.

> **Order Entry Example**
>
> **Current market price: 510 1/2**
> **Average settlent price: 480**
>
> **If you are buying,**
> **enter a market order**
>
> **If you are selling,**
> **enter a limit order**
> **if inside allowable trading range.**

If the prevailing market price is well under the average price on a buy or well over the average price on a sell, I will typically use a market order. If the market price is close to the average price, I will use a limit order at the average price to ensure that I do not enter the market on the "wrong side" of the average price. Keep in mind that a limit buy order entered above the market price or a limit sell order entered below the market price will both be filled at the prevailing market price.

What constitutes "near" historical highs or lows? This is one of the "artistic" components of seasonal trading. You will need to check historical levels as you approach each new trade possibility, and use your best judgment to determine if you're too close for comfort. If I am within a few ticks of an historical benchmark, I will look for another trade. Historical highs and lows are usually a tip-off that abnormal conditions are overwriting seasonal tendencies.

I suggest working with an account of at least $15,000 to $20,000 to comfortably trade this method. This should provide enough margin money to enable you to maintain an average of approximately 10 positions throughout the year, although this will vary based on the contracts you trade.

---

*I consider interest rate and indices trades as exceptions to criteria number one, due to the ever-changing values of the underlying instruments. These trades may be taken regardless of the relationship between average settlement price and current market price.

I've used this price comparison method to guide my seasonal trading since 1995. In 1998, I entered the Robbins Trading Company's prestigious *World Cup Championship of Futures Trading* for the first time and finished 2nd in my division with a 71% return. I placed among the top-10 finishers five of my first six years in World Cup competition, including a first-place finish among all competitors with a return of 595% in 2002 when I funded my account with $16,828 in January and ended the year with a balance of $100,180. As of press deadline for this article, I was leading the 2004 World Cup with a 426% return through 07-16-04, increasing my $15,000 opening account balance to $78,866 in six and a half months.

In this chapter, I've shared with you the same tools I've used to develop my extensive Blue Book of trade set-ups. You can develop your own personal notebook of trades by following the steps outlined in this chapter and using some basic programming skills.

One note of interest: Due to the "pedal to the metal" nature of the *World Cup Championship* and certain rules of the competition, I allow myself to occasionally veer from the aforementioned rules in my championship account only. For instance, I might enter a long position even when the current market price is above the average settlement price, or I might extend the window of market entry somewhat past the defined date. Until you have had considerable experience and success with my method, I highly recommend that you strictly adhere to the system parameters as outlined below.

EXPIRATION RULES:

Heating Oil/ Unleaded Gas	Last business day of the month preceding the delivery month
Natural Gas	Three business days prior to the first calendar day of the contract
Copper/Silver	Third to last business day of the maturing delivery month
Palladium/ Platinum	Fourth business day prior to the end of the delivery month
Grains (except soybean oil)	Business day prior to the 15th day of the contract month
Soybean Oil	Last business day prior to the 15th day of the contract month
Coffee	Eight business days prior to last trading day of delivery month
Cocoa	Eleven business days prior to last trading day of delivery month
Cotton	Seventeen business days from end of business month
Orange Juice	14th business day prior to the last business day of the month
Sugar	Last business day of the month preceding the delivery month
Live Cattle	Last business day of the contract month
Feeder Cattle	Last Thursday of the contract month
Pork Bellies	Four day before the end of the contract month
Lean Hogs	Tenth business day of the contract month

PART 3

CHAMPIONSHIP TOOLS FOR TECHNICAL TRADING

t's one thing to hear champion traders explain their methods. It's another thing entirely for those champions to share their tools. As the next two chapters will show, that's exactly what these top traders are doing. They are disclosing their tools, secrets, methodologies and techniques in detail to you. I can tell you from experience, only the most dedicated, committed and successful traders are willing to share their knowledge and expertise so openly.

In the next two chapters, World Cup traders John Mills and Robert Bloch explain the technical tools that they used in the championship and that they continue to use to this day. For Mills, a four-time World Cup trophy winner, the tool of choice is a Trading Equity Graph, which established his goals, monitored his progress and helped manage his capital. For Bloch, a multiple trophy winner with an unparalleled World Cup track record, it is an oscillator that he used to determine his trading entry and exit points.

No trading tool or trading system is foolproof, and World Cup traders would be among the first to admit that. But tools and systems are essential to any trader's success, whether trading a one-lot or managing a multi-million-dollar portfolio. Without a system and technical tools, trading is little more than hunches and guesswork. And, as I've seen far too many times over the years, those who claim to have a real "feel" for the market or who can make a trade just by "looking at a chart" are fooling themselves — but not for long. Their lack of discipline and technique will soon take them out of the game.

One of the most important lessons of these two chapters and of the entire book is that trading requires discipline and technique. Traders must have a firm rationale for where a trade is made and why it is being made. If those two questions can't be answered, then the trade isn't worth making. While systems can be elaborate and complex, they do not make trading more difficult. Just the opposite! Systems and technical tools make trading far more manageable, helping you to identify and confirm a trade — where to get in, where to get out, and where to put a stop. They reduce your risk and help preserve your capital.

Don't get me wrong. Trading isn't as easy as pushing a button. But it can be reduced to more basic elements that make it more manageable, especially for novices who are interested in trying their hand at it. To me, that's the appeal of Mills' Trading Equity Graph. He took a lofty goal — not just participating in the *World Cup Championship,* but actually winning a trophy in competition! — and broke it down to basic parts. He knew what he wanted to accomplish and what it would take to get him there. Using the Trading Equity Graph, he plotted what his return would have to be each month and each week. Then, with smaller, incremental goals, he developed a system that would enable him to reap his return objective with an appropriate risk.

As Mills explains, "Determining the end goal is essential before undertaking any business venture, and trading, after all, is a business and should be treated as such."

Mills accomplished his objectives, earning four Bull and Bear trophies for top-three World Cup performances between 1989 and 2000. Today, Mills is a Commodity Trading Advisor, based in Ohio, who trades a wide variety of futures products as well as the forex market.

Like most traders, Bloch tried out a variety of systems and oscillators over the years. Then he set about developing his own, looking for an oscillator that could work in any market — simply, efficiently and consistently — to determine and confirm the trend. As Bloch writes, "Finding a system that could easily determine the direction of the trend would greatly improve a trader's chances of making a profit trading commodities. Determining the trend is only the first step, however. A trader must also be able to enter trades when the chances are high for a successful trade."

The result of his endeavors is a tool he calls the Robert Bloch Triple Crossover Oscillator — or RBTC oscillator for short. In his chapter, Bloch shares the secret of this oscillator, including how it can be used in virtually any market, from the highly liquid S&P futures to the obscure milk futures. He attributes the RBTC oscillator with much of his success, including two of his World Cup trophies.

Bloch has enjoyed unparalleled success in the World Cup, including a 1999 victory in the non-professional division with a 179% return *and* a second-place finish in the professional division with a 216% return the same year. He placed at least two accounts in the World Cup Top 10 in four out of five years from 1998 to 2002, and has received a record six Bull & Bear trophies for top-three finishes in the World Cup. Today, Bloch is a Commodity Trading Advisor and manages a $50 million bond portfolio for a bank in California, where he resides.

For any trader, reading about the experiences of disciplined and technically minded traders is important. But to have the opportunity to look over the shoulders of trading champions as they walk through their rationale, methodologies and their successes and failures is an invaluable education.

CHAPTER 6

TRADING WITH AN EQUITY GRAPH

BY JOHN MILLS

First came the goal: To have a chance to win the *Robbins' World Cup Championship of Futures Trading*, I would need to make at least a 50% return on a $10,000 account. That meant I needed to make $5,000 by trading before December 31st.

Traders who set weekly, monthly or yearly goals for themselves will recognize this rationale. Whether trade is your sole income or supplements it, you know what you want to make over a specific time period. Once that goal is established, you can break it down further: by day and even by trade. For me, this was not an intellectual exercise; it was an important part of the development of my strategy and trading plan, which ultimately led to a respectable finish in the *World Cup Championship* with a return that was almost exactly what I had planned.

Thus, as I set my trading plan, I broke my $5,000 yearly goal into smaller increments: I needed to make $416.66 per month or $96.15 per week. That certainly sounded more attainable than a 50 percent return. Through this exercise, I defined my objective and established a weekly goal of making $96.15 per week. All I needed was a tool to keep me on track.

The Trading Equity Graph, as I call it, became the single most important tool I used during the *World Cup Championship*. It remains the most significant part of my trading today. Traders who use this tool will find it is more than just a performance-tracking device. As you'll see, the Trading Equity Graph also sets up profit targets and stop-loss points for each and every trade that you make.

The Trading Equity Graph

To make the graph, I simply took a sheet of graph paper with 52 squares, each representing one week. The X-axis was for money and the Y-axis was time in weeks. I drew a base line representing the starting point of $10,000. Next, I plotted a diagonal line from my starting date of January 1st to the ending date of December 31st. The line started at $10,000 and ended at $15,000, representing my objective for a 50% return on my account. As the line intersected each square, I could see my cumulative weekly goal — and judge my actual performance accordingly. Then I plotted another diagonal line from $10,000 to $20,000, representing a 100% return on my account. This process can also be done using software such as excel or access since daily data can be downloaded to the graph for daily equity chart updates. However, I still recommend updating the equity graph by hand each day as it forces you to stay a little closer to your positions and risk per trade then if you had automated.

Now it was time to think about risk. How much of my original $10,000 was I willing to risk? I believe that the minimum return-to-risk ratio should be at least 2-to-1. I chose 25% as my ultimate downside for the championship. Following this process, I drew a horizontal line from January to December at the $7,500 level. At this point, I had graphed my entire year before the fact. I knew where I wanted to go and where I would stop trading. I wanted to make a minimum of $5,000 and lose a maximum of $2,500. If I were fortunate enough to make 100% on my account, then my reward to risk would be 4-to-1.

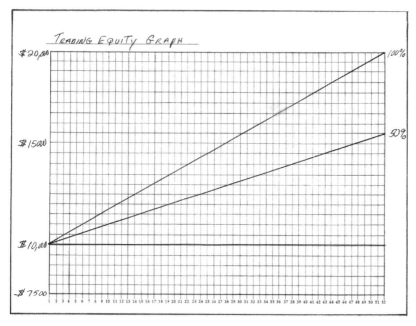

GRAPH 6.1   BASIC TRADING EQUITY GRAPH

CHOOSING A STRATEGY

With a means to track and control my trading, it was time to search for the best trading strategy. Before I could choose a strategy, method or system, however, I first had to ask myself: How much time did I have to devote to trading? At the time of the championship, I was president of a very fast-growing chain of hair salons, a position that required long hours in the office and many out of town trips each month. It became necessary to limit my research for a trading strategy to one that would fit my already busy schedule. At the time, access to data was nothing like it is today. There were no online websites providing real-time data or trading platforms. Real-time data could be obtained from satellite vendors, but for the most part these services were cost prohibitive for the small trader.

While data-access has changed today, traders still have to decide how much time — realistically — they have to devote to trading. If time is available during the day and trading does not interfere with other responsibilities, then you may choose to trade intra-day using real-time data. This opens the door to very short-term trading strategies using data tick-by-tick, 5-minute bar charts, and so forth. Traders must find a style and a strategy that reflects their goals, their lifestyle and commitment to trading, and even their personalities and temperaments.

As for me, given my other commitments, I had no choice but to find a system that used daily or weekly data. Interestingly, through the years since my first *World Cup Championship*, I still have the most trading success using daily and weekly data. I know many traders who trade only using intra-day data and they do very well. I have also developed systems for intra-day trading that looked good in back testing and on the charts, but they did not stand the test of time. Clearly, the timeframe that suits me best is one that uses daily and weekly data. But without examining my trading options in light of the realistic demands and other pressures on my time and energy, I could not have made this first determination.

TECHNICAL VS. FUNDAMENTAL TRADING

The next step was to determine my approach to the market. In other words, was I a technical or a fundamental trader? Once again, this is another basic question that all traders must ask themselves before adopting a specific trading approach or system. Both the fundamental trader and the technical trader seek to determine the future direction of prices, but their approaches are vastly different.

The fundamental trader/analyst searches for reasons for future price movements, and bases trading decisions upon those determinations. The technical trader studies price movements, assuming that all the known information influencing a particular commodity or market is reflected in the price at any point in time.

To illustrate this, a fundamental soybean trader may study crop reports, weather patterns, storage reports, and so on to determine future supply versus demand in soybeans. Based on a careful analysis of the fundamentals, the trader would either buy or sell soybeans. On the other hand, a technical soybean trader would use various charting tools such as trend lines, oscillators, moving averages, chart patterns, and so forth to make buy and sell decisions. It is not important to the technical trader to know why prices are moving up or down. Rather, he needs to know that prices are moving and, based on the indicators, where they are likely to go next.

My studies of trading systems and approaches led me to choose a technical approach for some very simple reasons. First, I was not in a position to know or have access to all of the information necessary to develop a fundamental strategy. Second, if I had access to this information it would probably be outdated by the time I received and analyzed it. Certainly, fundamentals do play an important role in the success of a technical trading system. In fact, fundamentals will eventually win out, and demand and supply will rule. The great weakness in fundamental trading, however, is determining the timeframe in which various supply/demand factors will affect prices. For me and most traders, the best approach is a technical one, relying on indicators and signals that evaluate the market moves and determine what is likely to come next.

A WINNING SYSTEM

Based on what I had determined thus far, I knew what I needed to make, how much risk I would take on, and the kind of approach I would choose. The next step was the development of a trading system. The system I eventually created was the result of researching, studying and back testing literally hundreds of systems and approaches. The process of reviewing and studying how and why others trade provided me with a foundation for the eventual evolution of my own approach to trading. I learned what I liked and what I didn't. Every piece of information sparked new thoughts and questions.

Learning from the success — and the mistakes — of others is an important lesson for all traders. And, just because a trading system suited one trader, it doesn't automatically mean it will be successful for you. It may take on too much risk, for example. Or, you could begin trading a system just as it enters a drawdown.

One of the other benefits of studying a wide variety of trading systems is that I began to get a feel for the individual commodities and futures markets. I had never traded soybeans, live cattle or pork bellies. Previously, my trading was limited to silver futures. After a time, seeing charts side-by-side and testing various systems on different markets, it became clear which overall approach was the most comfortable *for me*.

Based upon my studies, I developed a list of seven parameters that I wanted my system to contain:

1. **The system must be as mechanical as possible.**

2. **The system must identify the current trend.**

3. **The system must identify specific, repeating price patterns.**

4. **The system must identify specific entry points, profit targets and stop-loss points.**

5. **The system must be simple and not over-optimized. The system must limit drawdowns to an acceptable amount.**

6. **The system must be consistent with both long and short trades.**

7. **The system must allow me to trade within my time constraints.**

THE MECHANICAL SYSTEM

I chose to make my system as close to 100% mechanical as I could because I believed at the time that any trader who was not on the trading floor could not get a feel for market movements over a one- to two-day period. With a mechanical approach, I had the ability to sit down each evening and look at my charts to identify which markets formed the price patterns necessary for my system trades. Once the markets were identified, it was very simple to determine entry, stop-loss, and initial profit exit points. After that, it was just a matter of writing out my orders and entering them with the broker prior to the open the next day.

I must note here that to trade any system profitability the trades must be made. While that may appear to be obvious, traders need to understand what can happen when a system undergoes one loss, and then another and then another. Second-guessing sets in and, to avoid further losses, traders are often tempted to pick and choose among the system's trades in hopes of avoiding further losers and getting only winners. As soon as a trader starts to second-guess the system, the result is usually disaster. For a system's full potential to be realized, each trade must be made. That means not only the five losing trades in a row, but also the sixth trade that is so profitable, it makes up for the previous losses and then some.

The mental attitude that I have found most helpful is to imagine that I've been hired to trade the system. This makes me the employee and my boss (my money) has given me one duty: to make the trades that the system generates. If the boss comes in the next morning and I haven't done my job, I run the risk of being fired. (In my case, I have had to beg for my job back many times.) Seriously, whatever image or mental attitude you use, understand that when you start trading a system, you must be fully committed. A half-hearted attempt, second-guessing the system, or only taking a portion of the trades generated will more than likely yield a less than satisfactory result.

TRADING THE TREND

In trading, the technical theory is that there are two types of markets: trending or trading range. A trend trader assumes that the trend, up or down, will continue. Thus, the trader will only make trades in the direction of the trend. The trading range trader assumes that there is no prevailing trend or direction to the market and will make trades in either direction as the market becomes either overbought (a sell opportunity) or oversold (a buy opportunity).

The assumption that I made is that the market is always trending up or down. I do not try to pick tops or bottoms, but rather assume that the market is in a trend 100% of the time. When the market is in an uptrend, I will only buy; when it is in a downtrend, I will only sell. The following charts (Charts 6.1, 6.2, 6.3, and 6.4) show the prevailing trend identified in the British Pound and in soybean oil.

CHART 6.1 BRITISH POUND WEEKLY CHART WITH ARROWS INDICATING TWO TREND CHANGES FROM JANUARY 2002 THROUGH JUNE 2002.

CHART 6.2 BRITISH POUND DAILY CHART WITH ARROWS INDICATING WHEN REAL-TIME PRICE MONITORING WOULD BEGIN.

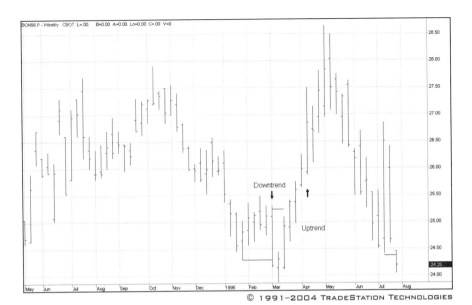

© 1991–2004 TradeStation Technologies

CHART 6.3   JUNE 1996 SOYBEAN OIL WITH ARROWS
INDICATING TREND CHANGES.

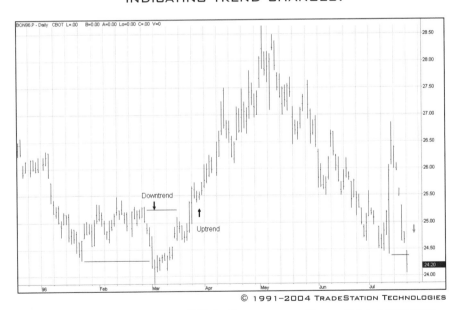

© 1991–2004 TradeStation Technologies

CHART 6.4   JUNE 1996 SOYBEAN OIL WITH ARROWS
INDICATING WHERE REAL-TIME PRICE
MONITORING WOULD BEGIN.

To establish the trend for any market, I follow the same approach. First, I use one weekly bar chart for each contract. Second, I determine the weekly pivot points, which represent the support and resistance levels. Weekly pivot points are the most recent weekly swing high or swing low on each respective chart. I then monitor daily prices to determine when a pivot point is broken. Once that happens, the trend has changed.

PATTERN RECOGNITION

Once a weekly support or resistance level is penetrated by daily price action (as seen in Chart 6.2) and a trend change has been indicated, it is time to watch for a trade to set up. In the World Cup competition, I set three parameters for entering trades. First, prices must form a short-term pivot point on the daily chart. Second, prices must retrace at least 25% of the difference between the daily pivot point high to the previous pivot point low. Third, there must be two consecutive lower highs.

There is no magic formula for determining the 25% used in this system. Percent retracement is a basic trading technique used over the years by many well-known and successful traders. What is important about using a retracement method is that it requires the price to come back to a support or resistance area before continuing the up or down trend. Keep in mind that I use this method as *one of three* parameters. This is an important distinction compared with systems that buy or sell at certain retracement levels.

Common retracement levels are 25%, 50%, and 75%, one-third, two-thirds and the Fibonacci ratios of 38.2 and 61.8. Whatever the level, when a pivot point is penetrated on a daily basis many resting buy (or sell) stops that are above (or below) the pivot point will be hit. This will likely accelerate the market in the direction of the new trend. Many times after this occurs, prices will retreat from these extreme short-term levels and consolidate for a few days. This is the period when traders are deciding if the pivot point penetration indicated a valid trend change.

For my purposes, the retracement represents the set-up for a buy (or sell) trade in the direction of the new trend.

ENTRY, STOP-LOSS AND PROFIT POINTS

Once the three parameters have been met, I know where I will place my buy or sell order and, if filled, my stop-loss exit order. If a new uptrend has been established, and I have two consecutive lower daily highs, I monitor the market on a real-time basis and wait for the price to penetrate the second day's high. When this occurs, I wait for the price to retreat by at least $150 below the second day high. (The $150 represents the highest amount of risk I was personally willing to take. This amount will vary by market and actual account size as well as acceptable risk exposure for different markets and traders. It is important to determine what level of risk you are willing to take.) If it does, I place a buy stop order at the second day high and, if filled, a protective sell stop at the second day high minus $150. The day order will be cancelled and replaced with the next day's high if it is lower than the second day's high and so on. Buy orders will be placed in this matter until it is either filled or prices penetrate the weekly low pivot point level establishing a down-trend. Then, of course, the process is reversed.

One cautionary note: If possible, wait until the market opens before entering orders to establish a trade. A gap opening above or below the entry price occurs very frequently and can result in prices far away from system entry prices. If the market gaps higher on the open, wait for prices to retreat before entering an order. If I get filled on a gap opening, I exit the position at the market, take my lumps, and wait for another trade to set up.

> "One cautionary note: If possible, wait until the market opens before entering orders to establish a trade. A gap opening above or below the entry price occurs very frequently and can result in prices far away from system entry prices."

Establishing Profit Targets

Establishing profit targets gets a bit more complicated. As I discussed in the opening of the chapter, my target was to make a net profit of $96.15 per week in order to realize my 50% annual profit goal. I had to add slippage and commission to this figure, resulting in a weekly gross profit target of a $150. During the *World Cup Championship*, I exited as near to a $150 profit as I could. Once the price moved above (below) my buy (sell) point, I grabbed as much profit as I could before prices retreated. In the majority of the trades early in the year, the penetration easily reached my $150 profit goal before prices retreated. Once I had built a comfortable profit, I was able to use slightly wider stops and stay with trades longer. The key, however, was to get out when the market moved the other way, knowing that there would always be another trade opportunity.

A few trades moved quickly to very good profit points, possibly $500 or $1,000, in just a few hours. Once I took these profits, my equity chart started to look very good. If I happened to make $1,000 in a day, I actually made enough money according to my equity chart to cover almost 10 weeks towards my annual profit goal.

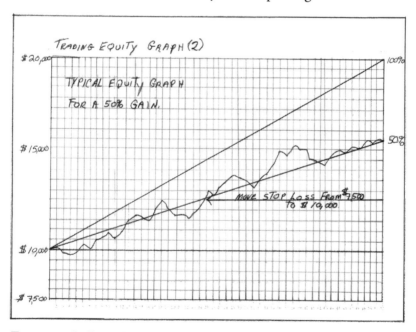

GRAPH 6.2   Typical Equity Graph for a 50% Gain

Using my Trading Equity Graph, my goal early in the year was to get my equity above the 50% line and keep it there. If it could reach 100%, it would be all the better. Once I had my equity comfortably above the 50% line, I could widen my stops and try to make a bit more per trade. The important rule, however, was that the 50% equity line became the absolute exit point for any trade, with the 100% line as a secondary profit target. If I was stopped out at the equity line, I resumed my original trading strategy until I had again built a comfortable profit above the equity line. At that point, I moved my ultimate stop-loss from $7,500 to $10,000. This created a breakeven situation for the year even if my system fell apart.

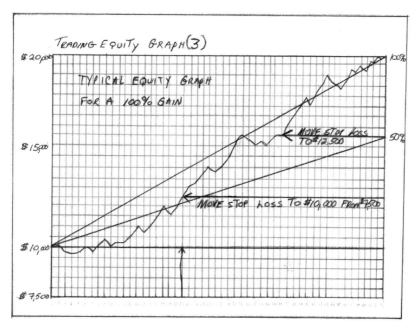

GRAPH 6.3   TYPICAL EQUITY GRAPH FOR A 100% GAIN

Furthermore, knowing my net profit goal per week, it was very simple to determine where my profit should be on any given day. For example, on the 24th week, I knew my net profit should be $961.15 × 24 or $2,307.60.

PUTTING IT ALL TOGETHER

The approach I used in the *World Cup Championship* has formed the foundation of my trading. For some traders, my specific approach may not suit their needs or their desire for more frequent intra-day trading. Nonetheless, I believe my systematic pursuit of a trading system that could meet my objectives can be helpful for any trader who is setting goals and devising a system.

Regardless of a trader's individual approach, there are two basic challenges in trading that are universal: One is creating a trading system that you believe in; the other is to understand and control yourself. Many traders find it easier to create a system than to trade it. I know several excellent system designers who have created very profitable systems but who cannot follow the system rules and trade their own systems successfully.

> **". . .there are two basic challenges in trading that are universal: One is creating a trading system that you believe in; the other is to understand and control yourself."**

Most beginning traders are more interested in the act of trading than in self-control. It is easy to stay with a losing trade too long. It is easy to take profits too early. Successful traders, however, have learned to control their fear, greed and ego in order to trade the approach that they believe in. Some learn easily and some may need to experience financial disaster before they finally get the idea. Others never learn and go from system-to-system, blaming the system for their losses without recognizing the problem lies within them. Good money management can make a mediocre approach profitable. Bad money management can turn the Holy Grail of trading into a losing proposition.

TRADING AS A BUSINESS

Trading is not different than any other business, which is one of the underlying principles of my Trading Equity Graph as a tool to determine objectives and plot progress. The entrepreneur who has an idea for a business venture must put together a very detailed business plan to turn it into reality. The same holds true for the full-time trader. The trader must do the necessary projections to determine if the venture will provide the necessary profit to support the lifestyle that he or she enjoys.

The great advantage to trading is leverage. In most cases starting a new business requires substantial capital just to get the doors open. With futures trading, a relatively small bankroll and a good system are all you need to get started. How long you stay in the business depends on the same attention to detail as in a normal business. The doors have to be open on time. In trading, that equates to making the trades. Expenses need to be kept to a minimum. That equates to money management. The expected profit margins must be realized. That means a system that works consistently. Losses should be put in the same column as investment capital for the ultimate success of the business. They are as much a part of the business as rent is for a retail store. Losses will occur. It's up to the trader to control the size of the losses.

> **Good money management can make a mediocre approach profitable. Bad money management can turn the Holy Grail of trading into a losing proposition.**

When starting a trading business, the Trading Equity Graph is a valuable tool to use to determine the type of system to trade and your financial requirements. In my case, I designed a system that I thought could make $5,000 on a $10,000 investment. To make $40,000, I would have had to invest eight times the initial amount or $80,000 to make a $40,000 profit. On the other hand, I could have designed a system that was more dynamic, taken larger positions, assumed more risk — or all of the above.

I found the Trading Equity Graph to be invaluable in the *World Cup Championship*, and I continue to use it today. For traders who sometimes become lost in the market, unsure of where they are or what they need to accomplish, this tool will help plot their desired course and chart where they are compared with their desired destination.

CHAPTER 7

THE TRIPLE CROSSOVER OSCILLATOR

BY ROBERT BLOCH

I n my career as a trader, I have evaluated many different systems and oscillators over the years. Displeased with the consistency of the methods I tried, I set out to develop my own oscillator. I wanted an oscillator that would be relatively simple, work in any market, and have the ability to catch large moves or identify the direction of the main trend. The result of my quest was my Robert Bloch Triple Crossover Oscillator (RBTC), which was instrumental in my *World Cup Championship* performance.

In this chapter, I will outline the development of the RBTC and explain how you can use it in your own trading. Before getting to that point, however, consider why traders use technical tools in the first place. As the old adage goes, "the trend is your friend." Finding a system that could easily determine the direction of the trend would greatly improve a trader's chances of making a profit trading commodities. Determining the trend is only the first step, however. A trader must also be able to enter trades when the chances are high for a successful trade. This requires a great deal of patience, which is difficult to maintain in the heat of the trading battle. But to lose patience can be very costly.

WAITING FOR THE SET-UP

If you feel the market is going to move higher and it takes off without you, you may panic and try to get on board, fearing you'll miss the whole move if you don't. More times than not, you'll regret not waiting for the trade to set-up, and find instead that you have entered the market prematurely — only to get stopped out for a loss. In trading, panic rarely leads to a good decision and impatience is not rewarded.

Remember, when you are on the sidelines waiting for the right set-up, you aren't losing any money. Rather, you are preserving your capital for the set-up that can make a large profit. Sometimes you don't get the set-up, and the trade takes off without you. It happens to every trader. Developing the techniques to identify the trade set-ups — and having the discipline to wait for them — will vastly improve your consistency in trading and your results.

The hardest part, I believe, is waiting for the set-up that never really materializes. Then you have to wait on the sidelines and watch the market do exactly what you thought it would — only you aren't participating. Here's a typical example:

> "Developing the techniques to identify the trade set-ups — and having the discipline to wait for them — will vastly improve your consistency in trading and your results."

My analysis on the 15-minute chart of S&P futures was that the market would trade lower for the day. I had taken on one short position the night before and was looking for an opportunity to add to it. My game plan going into the day was to short the market after it rallied, which would give me a low-risk entry point. The market never accommodated me and it never gave me the low-risk entry point that I was waiting for. It just drifted lower for the entire day. I could have made some money on this trade if I had gone with my original gut feeling. But I have found over the years that my technical indicators are more reliable, consistent, and more profitable than my gut feelings.

I also know that today is just one day out of the year, and if I didn't get a trade today, then I will wait for the next signal tomorrow. It's like the batter at the plate in baseball. Some of the most successful hitters go to the plate waiting for their favorite pitch and when it is served up to them, they hit it out of the ballpark. That is exactly what you want to do. Wait for the set-up, enter your trade, and go for the profit. You don't have to buy at the exact low or sell at the exact high. You only need to sell at an amount higher than where you purchased. Following this approach has allowed me to obtain consistent profits and, occasionally, very large profits. The point is the set-up is vital to the success of your trade. It is essential to have the right technical tools to identify how, when and where to enter a trade and exit the market with a profit.

THE ROBERT BLOCH TRIPLE CROSSOVER OSCILLATOR

One of my favorite tools is my Robert Bloch Triple Crossover Oscillator (RBTC), which is very easy to use. There are no complicated rules and you can typically review all of the major commodity markets in just a few meetings each night. The RBTC oscillator actually consists of two moving averages and a zero line ("0-line"). Moving averages have been around for a long time and many traders have used them with varying degrees of success. Many analysts don't like moving averages since they can be a lagging indicator: There's a chance that the market has already made a substantial move before the moving average indicates an entry point. Or, a moving average can be so sensitive that you get whipsawed and suffer several losses before you hit a good trade. To counter these drawbacks, I have found the interaction of the moving averages in relation to each other can present some very profitable opportunities. That's where the RBTC comes in.

I utilize a computerized trading program to calculate the moving averages for use in my oscillator. Rather than using a trading moving average (which calculates an average value over a fixed period of time), the RBTC uses an *exponential* moving average. An exponential moving average is calculated by adding a percentage of yesterday's moving average to a percentage of today's closing value. In this way, more emphasis is put on the most recent data and less weight on the oldest data. This makes the moving average more responsive. Once I have the exponential moving averages, I look at the two moving averages and their position relative to the 0-line. That generates the entry points based on my RBTC oscillator.

Before going any further on how the signal is calculated, it's important to understand how the RBTC oscillator works. As the charts on the following pages show, RBTC appears as a jagged line. When it crosses the horizontal line or 0-line, a change in the direction of the trend is indicated and a trade is initiated. This oscillator is primarily designed to identify the direction of the market's current trend. If the jagged line moves from below the 0-line to above the 0-line, the oscillator signals that the trend is now up, and you would want to play the market from the long side. You can use the crossover of the 0-line as your initial entry signal to go long.

If the jagged line moves from above the 0-line to below the 0-line, the oscillator signals that the trend is now down and you would want to play the market from the short side. You can use the crossover of the 0-line as your initial entry signal to go short. As the market moves up and down, you can then look for additional opportunities to enter trades in the direction of the trend. Often, there will be additional opportunities to add to your position or get on board if you missed the initial signal.

To understand how the RBTC oscillator can be used, I will discuss several different commodities such as the Swiss Franc, lean hogs, U.S. Treasury Bonds, S&P 500, and corn. And, just to show that my oscillator could work in any market, I will even look at an obscure market: milk futures. Very few traders actually trade milk. In fact, I personally, have never traded it. But if my system can work in a thinly traded, obscure commodity market like milk, then it can work in any other commodity.

Each of the following charts are from the same period of time and were current as of this writing. On occasion, I will zoom into a specific timeframe to demonstrate my other technique for entering a trade with my RBTC oscillator. This will show that I have not gone back in time just trying to pick out a few instances in the past where this system worked. Later in the chapter, I will discuss the same trades using additional techniques that would confirm or counter the initial signals, and also provide points at which to add to a position or enter a trade if the initial signal were missed.

Chart 7.1 shows the oscillator on a daily chart of the September Swiss Franc. Suppose you were bullish the Swiss Franc market and felt that the market would be improving and a low was imminent. This oscillator would have kept you from entering the market from the long side from January 2, 2002 through March 6, 2002. Just imagine how much money you could have saved by waiting for the oscillator to give a signal that an uptrend had begun! Better yet, what if you had shorted the market and waited until the trend turned upward?

CHART 7.1

Chart 7.1 shows a sell signal generated at Point A on January 2, 2002, at a price of 6031. After the sell signal was initiated, the market declined to a low of 5820 on January 31, 2002. The buy signal at Point B on Chart 7.1 was not generated until March 6, 2002 at a price of 5949. After the buy signal at Point B, the trend changed and the market moved substantially higher, putting in a high for this move on July 22, 2002 at a price of 6974. The next signal came on July 31, 2002, indicated as Point C at a price of 6731. This is where patience really pays off. The RBTC oscillator gave only three signals in this market for eight months, but look how profitable they were.

At times, this system does make it look very easy to find profitable trades. But no matter how good a system is, it will encounter losses. Losses are a natural part of trading and should be expected. The key is to keep your losses small and prevent them from destroying your capital. When trading the markets, it is always wise to place a stop loss after you enter a position. A stop will limit the amount of loss you could incur if the market moves against you, and prevent a losing trade from become a huge loss.

A trailing stop works much in the same way as a regular stop loss, except the stop is moved periodically in the direction of the market. This allows profits to continue to accumulate while still providing protection should the trend reverse. The trailing stop should be far enough away from the current price level to compensate for intra-day volatility as the price moves in the larger trend. Be sure to move the stop higher each time it is safe to do so.

Chart 7.2 illustrates the October lean hogs. Points A and C are sell signals and Point B represents a buy signal. The first sell signal at Point A was generated on February 12, 2002 at a price of 5197. After the sell signal, the market didn't bottom out again until June 11, 2002 at a price of 3650. A buy signal was generated at Point B on July 1, 2002 at a price of 4080. After the buy signal, the market reached a high on July 17, 2002 at a price of 4385.

CHART 7.2

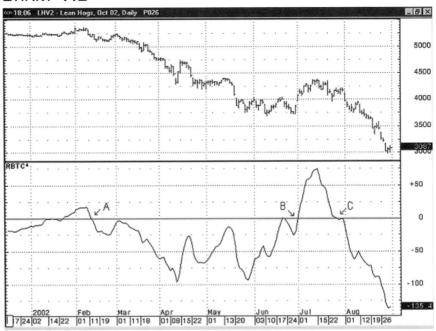

Traders cannot not expect to exit at the absolute high of every move, but a trailing stop will enable you to lock in a profit on a trade. In this case, Chart 7.2 shows the sell signal at Point C occurred on July 26,

2002 at a price of 4155. Since that sell signal, the market declined to a low of 2977.

Chart 7.3 shows the September U.S. Treasury Bond. There are four signals that the RBTC oscillator identified. The first signal occurred at Point A on March 4, 2002 at a price of 100 $^{21}/_{32}$. The market ultimately declined to a price of 96 $^{09}/_{32}$ on March 15, 2002. At Point B, the RBTC gave a buy signal on April 5, 2002 at a price of 99 $^{17}/_{32}$. The high after that buy signal occurred at 101 $^{30}/_{32}$ on May 1, 2002. But no system is foolproof. The sell signal at Point C occurred on May 15, 2002 at 98 $^{31}/_{32}$. The lowest low after the sell signal was at 98 $^{25}/_{32}$. This was a losing trade.

CHART 7.3

The low that was generated on this decline was actually a buying opportunity, shown on Chart 7.3 as Point D, which was made on May 28, 2002 at a price of 100 $^{11}/_{32}$. The high since that buy signal was 112 $^{12}/_{32}$. The potential profit that occurred after the buy signal at Point D would have made up for any loss that might have occurred on the losing sell signal.

Chart 7.4 shows the S&P futures September contract, depicting five signals. At the time of this trade, S&P futures had been in a large decline since March 2000. The RBTC oscillator gave three buy signals and only two sell signals in the period under review. On the surface, it sounds like we would have lost money utilizing my oscillator, but that was not the case. We would have been rewarded following the system even though there were more buy signals generated in the opposite direction of the main trend than in the direction of the major trend. A buy signal was generated at Point A on March 1, 2002 at a price of 1137.50. After the buy signal, the market peaked on 1179.10 on March 11, 2002. The maximum profit potential from this signal would have been $10,400 trading just one S&P contract. A trailing stop would have been able to lock in a nice profit and, even if you had waited for a signal in the opposite direction, this still would have been a winning trade.

CHART 7.4

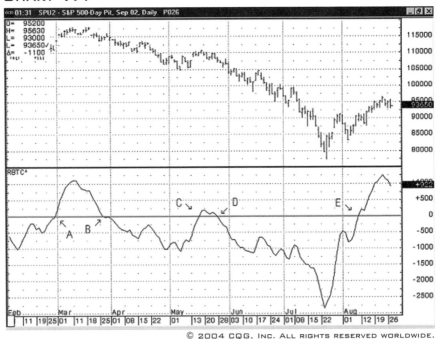

The S&P e-mini contract, which is 20% the size of the major S&P contract, allows traders to trade the S&P market on a smaller scale. I actually prefer the e-mini contract since I can sell five S&P e-mini contracts, which is the equivalent of an S&P major (same dollars at risk only slightly more commission). This gives me the added flexibility of being able to take profits on a portion of my position as the market moves in my favor, while retaining a partial position in the direction of the major trend.

Chart 7.4 indicates a sell signal was generated at Point B on March 27, 2002 at a price of 1148.50. After the signal at Point B, the market moved lower until May 7, 2002 when it attempted a bottom at 1048.00. The market gave a buy signal at Point C on May 16, 2002 at a price of 1100.60. The market only moved 10 points higher before the decline resumed. This would have been a losing trade on this buy signal because the market did not rally far enough to allow for a practical trailing stop. At Point D, the market gave a new sell signal at 1078.10. This losing trade would have resulted in a loss of about $5,625 on one S&P major contract. However, the gain from the previous trade of $11,850 would have more than compensated from this losing trade, resulting in a net profit overall.

Further, going short at Point D would not have been a bad trade. The market didn't hit a bottom until 773.00 on July 24, 2002. The last signal on Chart 7.4 was a buy signal indicated as Point E on August 9, 2002 at a price of 907.80. Going short at Point D until the buy signal at Point E would have resulted in a profit of $42,575 for each S&P major contract. Since the buy signal generated at Point E, the market rallied steadily, producing a winning trading, which would have been locked in by a trailing stop.

Chart 7.5 shows the December corn futures with three signals. First, there was a buy signal at Point A generated on May 8, 2002 at a price of 221 ¼. The rally up was short-lived and the market only moved up to 232.

Chart 7.5

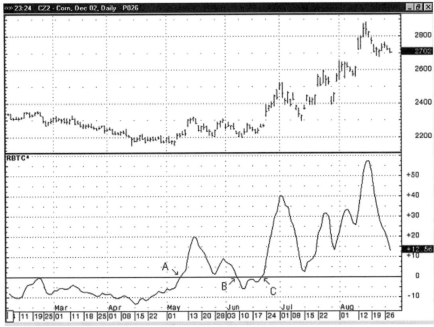

At Point B on June 10, 2002, the oscillator gave what appeared to be a sell signal. I say "appeared" because this trade would have been a loss. On June 21, 2002, a buy signal was received at Point C at a price of 226 ¾. The highest high of that move since the buy signal at Point C was 284.

Chart 7.6 depicts September milk futures. As I've said, I don't plan on trading this contract, nor do I recommend that you trade it. Nonetheless, let's take a look at how the RBTC oscillator works on this commodity. This chart had three signals. A sell signal was generated at Point A on April 12, 2002 at a price of 1339. The market then dropped until June 20, 2002 when it reached a low of 1100. On July 10, 2002, a buy signal was generated at Point B at a price of 1204.

CHART 7.6

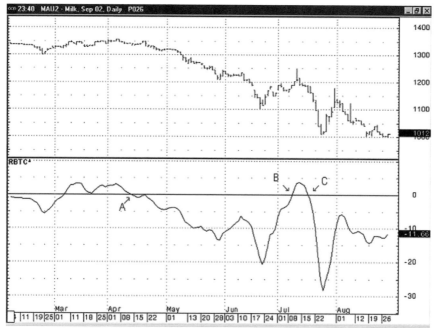

As you can see on Chart 7.6, this would have been a losing trade. On July 18, 2002, the market gave another sell signal at Point C at a price of 1163. The low since this last move has been 991.

FIBONACCI RATIOS

Traders, however, do not want to rely on just one indicator. To confirm or counter the initial signals I use another technique — Fibonacci ratios. I incorporate Fibonacci ratio analysis into my trading methodology to identify potential turning points. These points may signal the end of a move and therefore a point at which to take profits, or they may indicate a place at which to add to an existing position. In addition, if I missed the initial move or if I was stopped out because my trailing stop was too close, the Fibonnaci ratios may provide another chance to get into the market.

By using the Fibonacci analysis along with the RBTC oscillator, I can increase my chances of making a successful trade, avoid losing trades, and protect my profits by getting out at opportune times. Importantly, Fibonacci price areas also act as a kind of warning system against false signals, which can be generated by any trading system including the RBTC oscillator.

Fibonacci ratios are very popular in trading and many traders use these ratios for entering the existing markets. As a result of their popularity, Fibonacci price points are often where many traders put in buy/sell stops. Thus, these price points affect even traders that don't use Fibonacci numbers to trade because they tend to be important areas of market activity.

Fibonacci numbers, named for the 12th Century Italian mathematician, are derived from the sequence 0,1, 1, 2, 3, 5, 8, 13, 21, 34, 55, 89, 144, etc. Each successive number in the series is the sum of the last two numbers in the series preceding it. (Thus, 13 is the sum of $5 + 8$, and 21 is the sum of $8 + 13$.) The ratio between any two consecutively higher numbers in the series is .618 ($89/144$). The ratio of any two consecutive lower numbers in the series is 1.618 ($144/89$). Two other ratios that I use are the square roots of the first two. The square root of $.618 = .786$ and the square root of $1.618 = 1.272$. The fifth Fibonacci ratio that I use is .50.

To utilize the Fibonacci price ratios on a chart, the first step is to identify the high point and the low point. On Chart 7.7 for the September Swiss Franc, the low before the buy signal at Point B was generated is labeled as Point L1. The first high that was achieved after the buy signal is labeled as Point H1. After some profit-taking, the market drifted lower to Point S1, where the decline stabilized. Then the market was off on its way to a new high.

CHART 7.7

I have condensed the timeframe on Chart 7.7 to make it easier to see the Fibonacci analysis. Point L1 was the low on February 26, 2002 at a price of 5860. Point H1 is the high on March 15, 2002 at a price of 6060. The total initial rally from the low at Point L1 to the high at Point H1 was 200 points (6060 − 5860). To calculate the Fibonacci price ratios, multiply each of the five ratios (.5, .618, .786, 1.618, and 1.272) by the total move being analyzed. Then, subtract the product of the Fibonacci ratio times the total move 200 points (6060 − 5860) from the high to calculate each potential support line.

Applying the five Fibonacci ratios to the example produces the following results for a potential buying point:

$$[6060 - (.5 \times 200)] = 5960, [6060 - (.618 \times 200)] = 5936,$$
$$[6060 - (.786 \times 200)] = 5903, [6060 - (1.272 \times 200)] = 5806,$$
and
$$[6060 - (1.618 \times 200)] = 5736.$$

To assist you in calculating these points I have include a table below to illustrate the procedure:

Fibonacci Ratio		Total move High to low		Ratio times Total move	High		Ratio times Total move		Calculated Fibonacci Support
.500	×	200	=	100.0	6060	−	100	=	5960
.618	×	200	=	123.6	6060	−	124	=	5936
.786	×	200	=	157.2	6060	−	157	=	5903
1.272	×	200	=	254.4	6060	−	254	=	5806
1.618	×	200	=	323.6	6060	−	324	=	5736

As the market declines, support would be expected at or near each of the Fibonacci levels. Sometimes the market slightly overshoots the Fibonacci level, and sometimes it comes up short. This is not an exact science. It is only a trading tool. With that said, sometimes prices do stop exactly at one of the Fibonacci support or resistance levels.

As shown on Chart 7.7, the market found Point S1 at a price of 5950, which was between the .5 and .618 Fibonacci retracement levels. If you had already purchased a Swiss Franc on the signal at Point B (as indicated by the RBTC oscillator), you could have successfully added to that position at the Fibonacci support level. If you missed the first buying opportunity, this correction would have allowed you to get on board to enjoy a sizeable move.

Chart 7.8 for October lean hogs is an example of a sell signal based on the Fibonacci analysis. It is very similar to the buy signal shown on Chart 7.7 only this time the high is used as the first point and the low as the second point for construction of the Fibonacci resistance levels. Point H1 made on February 7, 2002 at a price of 5370, was the last high before the sell signal was generated at Point A. The first support for this market was on February 25, 2002 at a price of 5100. I have labeled this low as Point L1. With the high and the low points identified, the Fibonacci resistance levels can be calculated. The initial decline was 270 points (5370 − 5100). Applying the five Fibonacci ratios results in resistance/selling points as follows:

[5100 + (.5 × 270)] = 5235,
[5100 + (.618 × 270)] = 5267,
[5100 + (.786 × 270)] = 5311,
[5100 + (1.272 × 270)] = 5443,
    and
[5100 + (1.618 × 270)] = 5537.

High	5370
Low	5100
Total move	270

Fibonacci Ratio		Total move High to low		Ratio times Total move	High		Ratio times Total move		Calculated Fibonacci Resistance
.500	×	270	=	135.0	5100	+	135	=	5235
.618	×	270	=	166.7	5100	+	167	=	5267
.786	×	270	=	212.2	5100	+	212	=	5312
1.272	×	270	=	343.4	5100	+	343	=	5443
1.618	×	270	=	436.9	5100	+	437	=	5537

CHART 7.8

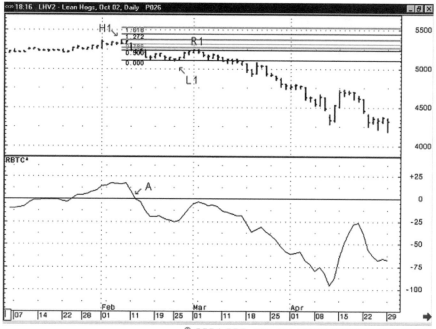

As Chart 7.8 shows, on March 4, 2002, the market rallied to a high of 5235 before running into resistance at Point R1. Resistance was expected here because of the .5 Fibonacci retracement ratio. After hitting this resistance point, the market continued lower as would be expected.

While Fibonacci ratios can pinpoint areas to establish a short or long position, this analysis isn't limited to the start of a move. There are times during an extended move, when Fibonacci ratios can keep you from exiting a position too soon or prematurely taking a position in the opposite direction. For example, as shown on Chart 7.9 for October Lean Hogs, Fibonacci ratios could have alerted you that a buy signal might fail and that the trend would again reverse to the downside.

CHART 7.9

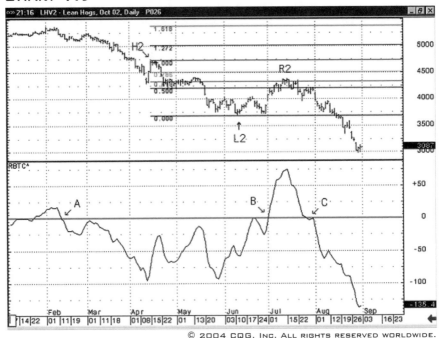

Chart 7.9 indicates that a new sell signal was generated at Point C. But what preceded that indicator? First, there was a sharp three-day rally that ended on April 16, 2002 at a price of 4735 at Point H2. On June 11, 2002, the market made a low at Point L2 at a price of 3685. The market then made a decent rally and generated a buy signal on July 1, 2002 at Point B at a price of 4080. The rally then topped out at Point R2 on July 15, 2002 at a price of 4385.

The move from point H2 to L2 was 1050 points (4735 _ 3685). Fibonacci resistance could be expected at 4334 [3685 _ (.618 _ 1050)] and at 4510 [3685 _ (.786 _ 1050)]. The high at Point R2 was very close to the .618 retracement and was in between .618 and .782. The decline that followed this failure at Point R2 was a down move that was worth catching, as the chart clearly shows.

Chart 7.10 for the September U.S. Treasury Bonds has several Fibonacci opportunities. Unlike other commodities, bonds trade in 32nds. Each 32nd is equal to $31.25. The low in this market, before the buy signal was generated at Point B, was on March 15, 2002 at a price of 96 $\frac{9}{32}$. This low is labeled as Point L1. The first high after the buy signal was Point H1 on May 1, 2002 at a price of 101 $\frac{30}{32}$, for a total up move of $\frac{181}{32}$. When applying the Fibonacci analysis to the bonds, you have to convert all calculations to 32nds. There is computer software that can automatically calculate the Fibonacci points using highs and lows. Or, you can calculate the Fibonacci points using a computerized spreadsheet program such as Lotus123 or Excel.

CHART 7.10

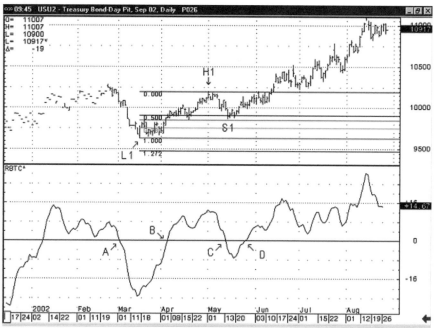

Fibonacci support would be expected to occur at 99 $\frac{3}{32}$ [101 $\frac{30}{32}$ − (.50 × $\frac{181}{32}$)] and at 98 $\frac{14}{32}$ [101 $\frac{30}{32}$ − (.618 × $\frac{181}{32}$)]. The low at Point S1 occurred on May 14, 2002 at a price of 98 $\frac{22}{32}$. This was in the range of the .618 and .5 retracements. After the market successfully held support at Point S1, it took off again to the upside.

Chart 7.11 for September bonds is another example of using a Fibonacci support point as a buying opportunity after the trend has been established. The low at Point L2 occurred on July 1, 2002 at 102 ^{08}⁄₃₂. The market had a sharp rally to a high at Point H2, which occurred on July 24, 2002 at a price of 107 ^{26}⁄₃₂. This was a move of ^{178}⁄₃₂. Point S2 represents the support levels for this market. The market bottomed out at 104 ^{10}⁄₃₂ on July 30, 2002. The Fibonacci .618 support level was at 104 ^{12}⁄₃₂ [107 ^{26}⁄₃₂ − (.618 × 178)].

CHART 7.11

The next two charts will show that Fibonacci ratios can also be used to identify areas for profit taking. Chart 7.12 indicates that the market for the September bonds hit a high at 105 ^{4}⁄₃₂ at Point H3 on June 26,

2002. The market declined for four days and bottomed at Point L3 on July 1, 2002 at a price of 102 $\frac{8}{32}$. The total move from Point H3 to L3 was $\frac{93}{32}$.

CHART 7.12

The resistance levels using Fibonacci analysis would be 105 $\frac{30}{32}$ [102 $\frac{8}{32}$ +(1.272 × $\frac{93}{32}$)] and 106 $\frac{30}{32}$ [102 $\frac{8}{32}$ + (1.618 × $\frac{93}{32}$)]. As Chart 7.12 shows, the exact high on July 11, 2002 at Point P1 was 105 $\frac{30}{32}$. In this case, the 1.272% retracement nailed the high to the tick. The market sold off for another four days before the rally resumed.

Chart 7.13 for September bonds again demonstrated how Fibonacci analysis can be used to take profits. From Point H4, which was also the profit high at Point P1, the market moved lower to Point L4. The price at H4 was 105 $\frac{30}{32}$ and the low at Point L4 was 103 $\frac{7}{32}$. The move down from H4 to L4 was $\frac{87}{32}$.

CHART 7.13

The resistance levels using Fibonacci analysis would be 106 $^{21}/_{32}$ [103 $^{7}/_{32}$ + (1.272 × $^{87}/_{32}$)] and 107 $^{19}/_{32}$ [103 $^{7}/_{32}$ + (1.618 × $^{93}/_{32}$)]. The subsequent rally up from Point L4 topped out at 107 $^{26}/_{32}$. This was close to the 1.618% retracement level. From that high, the market again declined for another four days until the rally continued again.

Fibonacci analysis is not limited to only daily charts, as shown in the previous examples. In Chart 7.14 for U.S. Treasury Bonds, the same analysis is applied to a weekly chart.

CHART 7.14

The market made a high at Point H5 the week of March 19, 2001 at a price of 107 $\frac{8}{32}$. It then declined to Point L5 the week of May 14, 2001 to a price of 98 $\frac{31}{32}$. The total decline from Point H5 to Point L5 covered a span of $\frac{265}{32}$. From the low at L5, the market had a huge rally up to Point P3 during the week of October 29, 2001 at a price of 112 $\frac{24}{32}$. The move up from the low at Point L5 to the high at Point P3 at 112 $\frac{18}{32}$ was a total advance of $\frac{435}{32}$. Where was the Fibonacci resistance? The 1.618% resistance level was at 112 12.32 [98 31.32 _ (1.618 _ $\frac{265}{32}$)].

Chart 7.15 for U.S. Treasury Bonds also utilizes a weekly chart, but this time the timeframe is expanded.

CHART 7.15

The market made a low at Point L6 at a price of 89 $\frac{9}{32}$, then rallied to Point H6 high the week of October 29, 2001 at a price of 112 $\frac{18}{32}$. The up move covered $\frac{754}{32}$. If you recall from Chart 7.14, this is the level at which we took profits from the rally that began the week of May 14, 2001. The market made a low at Point S3 on the week of March 18, 2002 at a price of 97 $\frac{16}{32}$. The total decline was $\frac{482}{32}$. The Fibonacci support at the .618% support was 98 $\frac{9}{32}$ [112 $\frac{18}{32}$ − (.618 × $\frac{754}{32}$)]. As Chart 7.15 shows, a long position established at that Fibonacci support would have been very profitable.

Fibonacci analysis, coupled with the RBTC indicators, works in the actively traded markets such as lean hogs, corn, Swiss francs, and U.S. bonds. What about milk futures? Can this analysis be applied to this thinly traded market as well?

Chart 7.16 of the September milk futures shows sell signal at Point A, generated on April 12, 2002 at a price of 1339. The high before the sell signal was at Point H1 at a price of 1356. The low came in at Point L1 on June 20, 2002 at a price of 1100. This was a decline of 256 points. The market rallied up to Point R1 on July 11, 2002 at a price of 1250. The Fibonacci resistance at .618% was at 1258 [1100 + (.618 × 256)]. The Fibonacci analysis once again successfully showed where resistance would be encountered.

CHART 7.16

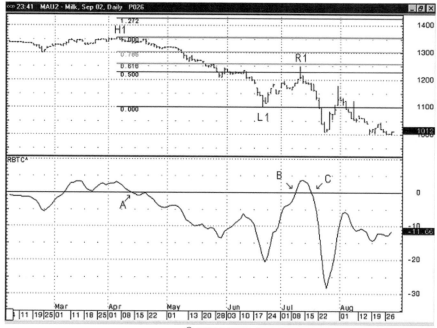

A buy signal, however, was generated at Point B (as shown earlier in the chapter). Given the nearby Fibonacci resistance level, this buy signal would have been viewed cautiously. And, as the chart shows, the subsequent sell signal at Point C led to the lower prices as the downtrend continued.

ROBERT BLOCH TRIPLE CROSSOVER OSCILLATOR (RBTC) CONSTRUCTION

With an understanding of what the RBTC oscillator can do, it's time to look at the parameters used to calculate it. I use the difference between two moving averages to construct the RBTC line. The computer calculates an 8.4 bar exponential moving average of the trend, and then subtracts from that moving average a 14 bar exponential moving average. The result is plotted. If the oscillator moves above the 0-line, a buy signal is generated; if it moves below the 0-line, a sell signal is generated.

Developing the RBTC oscillator, I tried numerous combinations. Finally, I found combinations that were sensitive enough and would get into the market early enough to catch a move before too much of the move had passed, but slow enough to try and avoid the whipsaws that would be encountered if the oscillator was too sensitive.

In 1998, after developing and implementing this oscillator, I finished third in the *Robbins' World Cup Championship.* I also received a first place trophy in the Robbins 1999 competition. Does this oscillator always work? No, it will encounter losses because no system is perfect, but as long as the gains exceed the losses, I am pleased.

As these results have shown, I believe the RBTC oscillator, used in conjunction with a second indicator such as Fibonacci analysis, is a powerful trading tool. Instead of relying on only one indicator to determine trade entry and exit points, the objective is to find a consensus of opinion from two or more techniques. When the indicators are in agreement, you can not only trade with greater confidence but reap potentially higher profits as well.

PART 4

Winning Strategies from a World Cup Advisor

I wish I had a dollar for every time a trader said to me, "I have a great system. It's been working like a charm. But I need something that will work in today's increasingly volatile and shorter-term markets." Wouldn't it be great to have a tool, an indicator or a method that shows you when to make your moves?

Enter WorldCupAdvisor.com staff member, Austin Passamonte, a Commodity Trading Advisor in New York, who weighs in with his favorite trading strategy — swing trading. This is a very hot topic for all traders, from those who day-trade to those who to take longer-term, buy-and-hold positions. It's all about timing: knowing when to get in and knowing when to get out — or when to hedge a position.

By definition, swing trading seeks to identify and capitalize on short-term corrections or "swings" against an underlying market trend. As he writes, "...knowing exactly when to buy, sell or hedge are the most vital steps to creating your financial future. With that in mind, a swing trading approach, using signals to know when to buy and when to sell, will play an important role in empowering you in your decisions."

With his unique approach, Passamonte takes on the most difficult and universal questions that every trader asks: When do I get in a trade? When do I get out? What happens when my system doesn't work well any more?

With his knowledge and expertise, this trading veteran provides you with the answers.

CHAPTER 8

SWING TRADING FOR SUCCESS

BY AUSTIN PASSAMONTE

Timing the market through a systematic approach known, as swing trading is an essential strategy for both the trader and the active investor. Understanding swing trading — in particular how it can identify trading opportunities in both trending and rangebound market conditions — is a plus for any trader, regardless of his or her style or timeframe. Swing trading concepts can also be applied by those who take longer-term positions in a stock or a particular market. Rather than buying and holding on, swing trading shows you when the market has run out of steam and it's time to take profits and bail out.

> "A common misconception is that buy-and-hold investing with stocks over the long haul is superior to market timing."

A common misconception is that buy-and-hold investing with stocks over the long haul is superior to market timing. It is true that during the past two decades of the greatest bull run seen to date, buy-and-hold investing made many people wealthy. But what happens when the market goes nowhere at all? How do you profit by holding a $20 stock when it's still trading around $20 years later? Impossible? Let's take a look at some recent moments in market history.

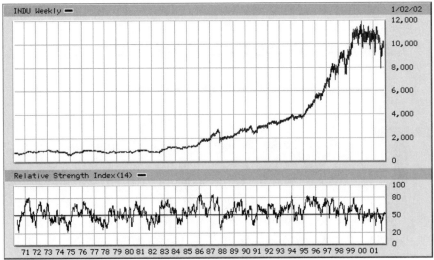

Chart 8.1   Dow Performance 1970–2001

As Chart 8.1 shows, the period from 1970 to 1983 saw the Dow go practically nowhere at all. From 1987 to 1995, the Dow traded within a 2,000 index-point range or double its value. Early 1997 into 2002, the Dow traded between 8,000 and 12,000 — by far the majority of that time was spent between the 10,000 and 11,000 levels.

Could the Dow double again? Will it go from 10,000 right now to 20,000 in eight years like it did before? Possibly. Will the Nasdaq swell to all-time highs in this same period or any similar? Possibly. But isn't it also true that both major indexes could just as easily move sideways in their present ranges for several years to follow? Absolutely.

Now, consider what can really happen when you "buy and hold" even over the long haul. The following examples are household name stocks, all of which had their heydays of investor fever when it was believed that the sky was the proverbial limit. No matter where you got in, regardless of what price you paid, there was a profit to be made in these stocks. At least, that's what investor behavior at the time seemed to indicate. Far too few people stopped to question if the stocks had already enjoyed their runs and, more importantly, if they should be looking for a place to get out, take profits, or at least hedge their holdings.

© 2004 QUOTE LLC. ALL RIGHTS RESERVED. QCHARTS™ IS A TRADEMARK OF QUOTE LLC, A
LYCOS NETWORK COMPANY. ALL OTHER TRADEMARKS SET FORTH HEREIN ARE OWNED BY THEIR
RESPECTIVE OWNERS. THE INFORMATION SET FORTH IN THIS SCREEN SHOT IS HISTORICAL DATA
ONLY, AND NOT CURRENT INFORMATION.

CHART 8.2 (TOP) AND CHART 8.3 (BOTTOM)
WEEKLY CHARTS FOR KODAK (SYMBOL EK) AND XEROX
(SYMBOL XRX)

BUY-AND-HOLD FALLACY

Kodak (see Chart 8.2) was once the world leader in film and photography production. One of the bluest blue chips fit for the proverbial widows and orphans, few other stalwart companies rivaled its solidarity. One of the few that did was Xerox (see Chart 8.3), which boasted world dominance in the photocopy and reprint industry. They were two thriv-

ing behemoths that could never feel the squeeze of adversity, and no analyst ever issued a sell signal on either of these until late 2000.

Thousands of lifelong employees still hold their entire retirement
plan in either of the stocks of the companies for which they toiled all
their lives. Has buy-and-hold, without the possibility of selling or hedging, secured their futures? Don't you think a gut-wrenching number of
retired employees have seen their comfort and security rise on paper only
to plummet right before their terrified eyes? Massive wealth was right
there on their monthly statements time after time, but without the
knowledge of simple hedging or exit strategies it has since turned to dust.

CHART 8.4 (TOP) AND CHART 8.5 (BOTTOM)
WEEKLY CHARTS FOR CORNING (SYMBOL GLW) AND INTEL
(SYMBOL INTC)

Similarly, not a single soul wanted to sell Corning Glassware Corp. (see Chart 8.4) during "fiber fever" in 2000, and more investors bought in the upper one-third of historical stock value than the lowest one-third. How many of these hapless victims would like to have used some simple hedge or exit strategies between then and now?

CHART 8.6 (TOP) AND 8.7 (BOTTOM)
WEEKLY CHARTS FOR SUN MICROSYSTEMS (SYMBOL SUNW) AND CISCO (SYMBOL CSCO)

Technology hounds figured, Sun Microsystems (see Chart 8.6) and mighty Cisco Systems (Chart 8.7) were the new blue chips on the block. These Nasdaq 100 heavyweights created numerous paper millionaires in their heyday. For a brief time in 2000, Cisco was the world's largest company by capital valuation. Talk of selling or hedging positions in either would get you flamed to ash in a chatroom for even suggesting such ludicrous ideas.

CHART 8.8 (TOP) AND CHART 8.9 (BOTTOM)
WEEKLY CHART FOR AT&T (SYMBOL T) AND POLAROID
(SYMBOL PRD)

AT&T, also known as Ma Bell (see Chart 8.8), was once the world's largest corporation, the first $100 billion dollar company ever. It enjoyed total domination in its industry with global reach and a diversified product outlook. Analysts and advisors would tell anyone to buy-and-hold this stalwart forever. No sell suggestions were ever issued by anyone on the Street until late 2000 or beyond.

Polaroid (see Chart 8.9) was a high-flyer in its day, part of the "Nifty Fifty" crowd from our last speculative bubble prior to the 1999 event. Buy-and-hold investors did great in this one for decades, but if they didn't sell before mid-1998, it was all a waste of time, money and effort.

CHART 8.10 (TOP) AND CHART 8.11 (BOTTOM)
WEEKLY CHART FOR QUALCOMM (SYMBOL QCOM) AND WORLDCOM (SYMBOL WCOM)

Qualcomm (see Chart 8.10) once reached $200 (adjusted for splits), and analysts gave a strong buy recommendation right at the pinnacle with a target of $250 per share next. Huge volume rushed in at the top when they beat the Street and were upgraded by numerous brokerage house analysts. Those who heeded what turned out to be poor advice and held from there are now down 75% and praying for a return to break sometime within the next decade ahead.

WorldCom (see Chart 8.11) was considered the next 800-pound gorilla in communications poised to conquer the world. Strong-buy market calls on the stock were issued every month but never a single sell suggestion until it was far too late. Then again, exit strategies weren't a major focus on Wall Street at the time. Sometimes, capital gains tax is cited as a reason to hold instead of selling. Another common justification is that if you invested in a company for a reason and that reason hasn't changed, then you should hold fast.

The second reason is an easy one for me to address. I buy any stock because I think its price is headed higher. If price action falls to a certain extent below my entry, the reason for me to invest in the first place no longer exists. Now, it's time to exit or at the very least hedge my position.

When it comes to tax consequences, the decision to exit is tougher, but there does come a point when this consideration is irrelevant. Investors who held countless stocks from highs of 1999–2000 down to the depths of 2001, saw their share value shaved by 75% to 90% or more of their original value. I'm no tax expert by any means, but I cannot envision why, when a stock is down 50% from the purchase price, exiting those trades would not have been a fiscally prudent thing to do. And selling to exit for any short-term gains at all versus a loss of 90% sounds mighty good to millions of retail investors right now, tax consequences be darned!

THE TRUTH USUALLY HURTS

Looking ahead to 2010 or beyond, no one knows what market scenario will play out. Granted, most people would love to think the market could double in value and would soundly reject the possibility of it moving sideways. The reason? It is just too painful to consider. Too many investors and traders are married to the myth that market wealth is easy, and time heals all wounds.

One thing I do know for sure is that the ability to buy a good market of any kind when its price is headed higher has never been a wasted skill. Likewise, the ability to exit or better yet short a market going lower will never be a wasted skill either. What's needed are simple, basic methods for buying low, selling high and selling high, buying low as market conditions mandate. The timeframe in which this may happen is irrelevant. It could be months, weeks, days, or hours as personal choice dictates. Regardless of how long, the basic method remains the same.

An Introduction to Swing Trading

Whatever your market outlook or your investment timeframe, I believe swing trading is an important strategy to incorporate. It plays to the market's natural short-term corrections or swings versus the underlying trend. After all, nothing goes straight up or straight down for long without at least momentary pauses or corrections before resuming the predominate move.

During the lifespan of an uptrend, it's inevitable some profit taking will occur along the way. Downtrends commonly move more in a straight line than rallies do because of underlying fear as traders storm the exits. However, even the most ferocious plunge is subject to relief rallies along the way, as profitable shorts cover their positions and dip buyers step in to look for bargains at lower levels.

Using multiple timeframe charts allows us to identify many of these market turns before or at the time they begin. You can time your entries to take advantage of moves and counter-moves to capture small profits repeatedly. This method is very subjective, and it takes time to study and perfect your chosen target market and technical signals.

Short-term trading is tougher than long-term investing, merely because decisions and market action are compressed into smaller windows of time. Investing or buy-and-hold trading are very deliberate, while day trading is hyperactive and/or pinpoint precise in execution. Swing trade methods lie somewhere in the middle.

It would easily take 200-plus pages to cover the broad outline and flesh out the detailed nuances of swing trading. However, that is not my intent. Instead, I will focus on the overall approach that works for me and numerous other traders, which should offer a firm base that you can mold to suit your personal style.

IDENTIFYING THE TREND

If a market is rallying and forms a defined upward trend on its weekly chart, the highest odds approach is to ignore short-play signals on intra-day charts and wait for pullbacks to get in on the dips. Likewise, markets spiraling downward in trend are not the most favorable for call plays. Instead, it's better to wait for the trend to flatten or reverse to the upside before initiating bullish trades. During times when underlying markets are rolling sideways without defined direction, traders can readily play long and short with equal degrees of success.

I prefer to rely on a small array of signals available to everyone. Stochastic values, trendlines, and chart patterns comprise the bulk of my directional assessment of the markets. I begin with oscillators such as stochastics, and determine if a market has bullish or bearish pressure at any given time.

CHART 8.12   WEEKLY CHART FOR INTEL (SYMBOL INTC)

In looking at Chart 8.12, note how the price action coils sideways while its stochastic readings are near an overbought extreme. You can see a bearish crossover as the fast-line turns down into the slow bar to indicate lower price levels ahead. This is a classic example of a short or put-play set-up. Stochastic fast and slow lines are above 80% overbought extreme and are both crossing over and curling down in weakened or bearish fashion.

This does not guarantee the price action will plunge straight down, nor does it mean the next move for these signals will be straight into oversold extreme. It does indicate that downward pressure is present and building for now, and the path of least resistance is continuing lower. Taking a trade in this direction has the greatest chance of success, while oscillator signals continue to trek lower.

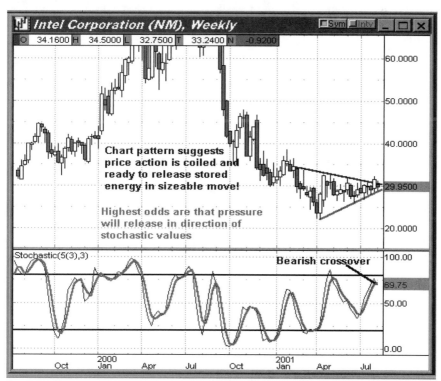

CHART 8.13   WEEKLY CHART INTEL (INTC)

Adding trend lines, the formation becomes a neutral wedge. Price action has coiled into lower highs and higher lows. Pressure has mounted and will be released soon. Which way? You never know for sure, but with stochastic values near overbought and looking bearish, they tip the scales that lower prices are in store.

CHART 8.14   DAILY CHART INTEL (SYMBOL INTC)

A daily chart gives a bigger picture for this same wedge formation. A one-day gap higher resulted in a lower session next and a gap down into the chart pattern again. This in itself is a clear bearish warning of a blow-off top. A break below the wedge pattern would confirm weakness is at hand. With stochastic values turning bearish once more, playing the downside is the high-odds bias.

© 2004 QUOTE LLC. ALL RIGHTS RESERVED. QCHARTS™ IS A TRADEMARK OF QUOTE LLC, A LYCOS NETWORK COMPANY. ALL OTHER TRADEMARKS SET FORTH HEREIN ARE OWNED BY THEIR RESPECTIVE OWNERS. THE INFORMATION SET FORTH IN THIS SCREEN SHOT IS HISTORICAL DATA ONLY, AND NOT CURRENT INFORMATION.

CHART 8.15   DAILY CHART INTEL (INTC)

As Chart 8.15 clearly shows, more downside was indeed in store. Traders, who went short Intel shares, call options, or Semiconductor HOLDR (SMH) shares, based on these simple tools did very well over time. Investors and traders who were long the stock or call options likewise had all kinds of time and preparation to hedge and protect their positions. Swing traders, on the other hand, would merely target downside plays while ignoring the upside as long as weekly/daily chart stochastic values rolled down.

Bullish Reversal

The exact opposite is true for swing trade call (long) plays. Here's a classic example of a long or call-play set-up. Chart 8.16 shows stochastic fast and slow lines are above the 80% overbought extreme and are both crossing over and curling down.

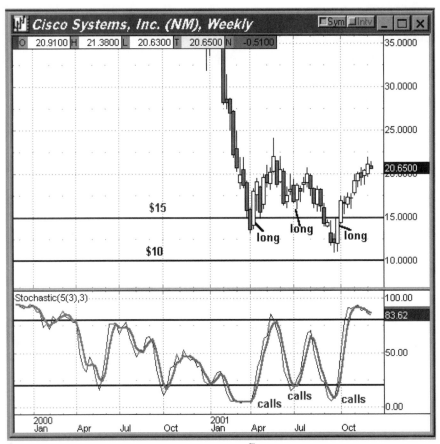

Chart 8.16   Weekly Chart Cisco (CSCO)

The Cisco weekly chart shows three defined rally periods in 2001, during which the stock rallied by $10, $4 and $9 respectively. These were all lucrative potential gains for such a low-priced stock. It's certainly possible that sideways rolling patterns can now be expected for this and similar stocks due to a massive overhead supply that's likely to suppress price levels for years to come. Following weekly chart signals may be the primary, if not the only way, to lock in gains during this decade.

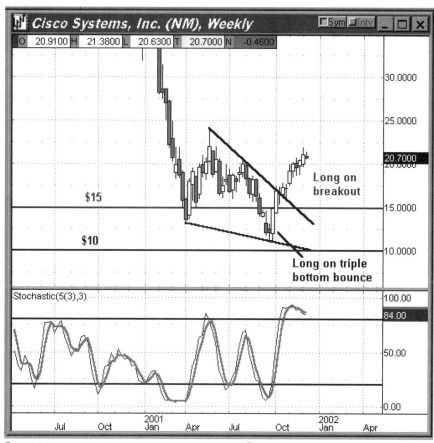

CHART 8.17   WEEKLY CHART CISCO (CSCO)

Adding trend lines, as price action permits, over a period of weeks allows you to monitor areas of resistance and support. In Chart 8.18, observe how price action behaves near these key points in harmony with or in opposition to stochastic values. This will indicate whether a current trend move is likely to continue, stall or reverse.

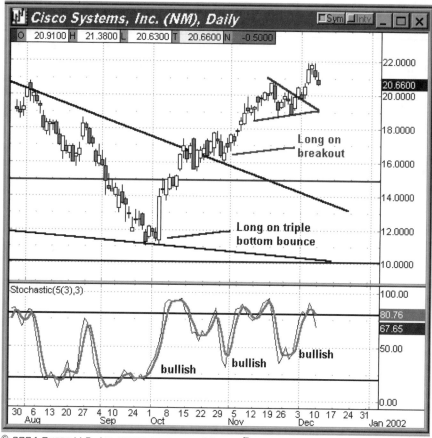

CHART 8.18   DAILY CHART CISCO (CSCO)

Weekly charts are the wide-view picture window to the trend, while daily charts define which way trend direction is currently moving.

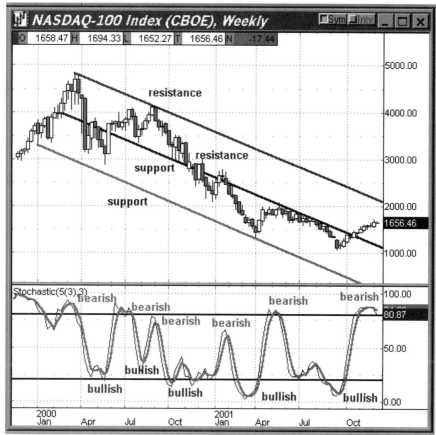

CHART 8.19   WEEKLY CHART NASDAQ 100 (NDX)

As Chart 8.19 illustrates, highly liquid, large float markets quite often follow a trend up or down within defined channels. Of course, it takes a couple of bounces up and down before anchor points to identify channels develop. Once that happens, trend lines can be extended to help identify future support and resistance.

Using plain trend lines or channels in conjunction with stochastic values or other oscillators gives two different technical measures to assess possible pivot points (see Chart 8.20). Note that where stochastic lines turned from oversold or overbought extremes in the same place, the price action touched lower, middle and upper channel lines. Each time you receive a dual confirmation of oscillator direction reversal along with a break of current support or resistance, you have high-odds proof that the market is about to change direction.

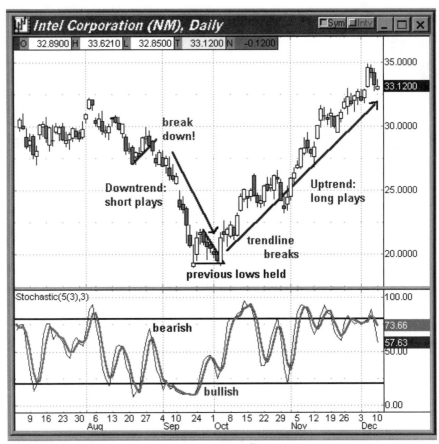

CHART 8.20   DAILY CHART INTEL (INTC)

Again, judging near-term market direction using daily charts along with simple studies such as trend lines, price patterns and price oscillators allow traders to remain on the right side of the market. Your goal should not be trying to catch each directional turn, but to follow the prevailing direction while picking off high-odds countermoves as they inevitably occur.

ENTRY AND EXIT SET-UPS

I use an entry and exit template for deciding when market moves are ripe for plays. As a short-term trader, it's imperative to study 60- and/or 30-minute chart signal alignments for precise entry, but there can be drawbacks to that as well. Time horizon, account size and risk level all play a role in determining where to enter a trade.

CHART 8.21   DAILY CHART SEMICONDUCTOR HOLDR (SHM)

The Semiconductor HOLDR (SMH) mirrors the Semiconductor Index (SOX) and its usual volatility. Chart 8.21 depicts the early April 2001 stochastic low and the first bull flag that was confirmed with a gap up open. Following that, a series of flags can be seen "walking" up this chart in staccato. Note that buying the open of each gap move was not the ideal entry: Lower prices followed immediately after. If you had used stochastic values to enter bullish trades and kept an eye on bull flag formations, which would have given you confidence to stay with this play, you could have ridden the move up from $35 to the $50+ area for a +40% gain within three weeks. I've worked longer for less than this buy-and-hold play could have yielded.

© 2004 QUOTE LLC. ALL RIGHTS RESERVED. QCHARTS™ IS A TRADEMARK OF QUOTE LLC, A LYCOS NETWORK COMPANY. ALL OTHER TRADEMARKS SET FORTH HEREIN ARE OWNED BY THEIR RESPECTIVE OWNERS. THE INFORMATION SET FORTH IN THIS SCREEN SHOT IS HISTORICAL DATA ONLY, AND NOT CURRENT INFORMATION.

CHART 8.22   DAILY CHART NASDAQ TRACKING STOCK (QQQ)

The NASDAQ Tracking Stock (QQQ) tells a similar story, as the SOX has a great influence upon the NASDAQ 100 (NDX). In Chart 8.22, QQQ shares near $35 would have reached the $50 area soon thereafter. The same bull-flag confirmation can be seen here as with the SMH. The ideal play would be to buy QQQ buyers on the next dip of the 60- and/or 30-minute chart stochastic values.

Take note of the series of false buy signals in early and late March when the slow stochastic bar broke above 20% oversold in bullish mode only to roll over again. Would you have gotten killed on early entries there? Not at all! Both were near the $40 area and a long buy still held up. This was exactly when some analysts were calling for the NDX to test the 1,000 level or roughly 25 in the QQQs. No one wanted to be a buyer at precisely this time, although hindsight shows this was the perfect time to buy.

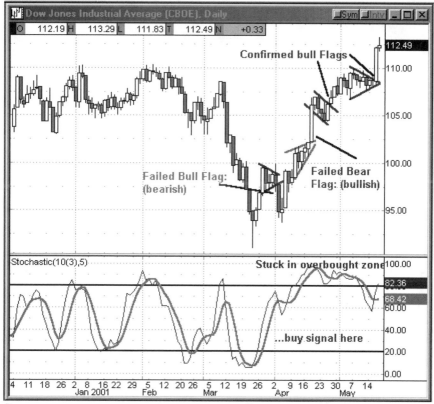

CHART 8.23   DAILY CHART DOW

Taking a look at the Dow next, observe in Chart 8.23 that if you had bought this index in late March when both stochastic values turned straight up, it would have been near the $96 range. Then a bullish flag broke to the downside and spooked longs for one scary day, until prices bounced and moved higher from there. Those who held long positions would have seen an ascending bearish pennant break to the upside, a failure that's very bullish by nature. Confirmation followed with another bull flag and a neutral wedge.

Buy-and-hold investors who merely stake positions when stochastic values emerge from oversold extremes and hold their positions until a bearish confirmation shakes them out, really do not need to know much more than this for picking trades.

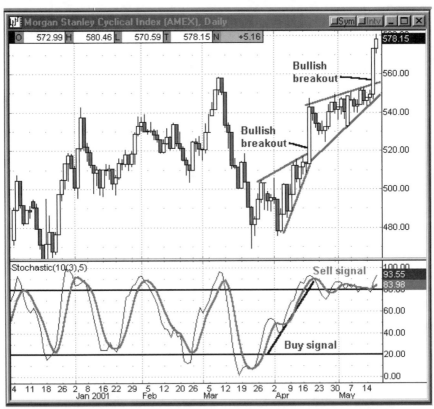

CHART 8.24   DAILY CHART MORGAN STANLEY CYCLI-
CAL INDEX (CYC)

Now we add iShares (IYC) and SPYDRs (XLY) to the game. To buy stocks, shares, future-month options, or Long Term Equity Anticipation Securities (LEAPs), look for the follow signal sequence:

1. **Both stochastic lines are at or within 20% oversold extreme.**

2. **Fast stochastic bar (bold line) crosses up through slow bar (thin line).**

3. **Slow bar (thin line) breaks 20% oversold and moves higher from there.**

Traders who want to be more precise can switch to 60- and/or 30-minute timeframe charts and enter long when these stochastic signals also align in oversold. There is nothing wrong with adding Bollinger Bands, various moving averages or any other confirming technical study. This is the base of what investors can do, and any number of additions can be made from here. I don't think more is necessary but surely cannot hurt either.

These are examples of high-odds trade entries with some of the best set-ups a trader could hope for. The next question, however, is when will profit targets be reached? If only the picture was always so clear. When you're trading, you don't have the luxury of hindsight. The easy answer is to wait for each and every signal to be clearly confirmed. There are times when you will need to anticipate the action based upon "feel," which I believe, is the result of studying particular markets for so long that you get a sense for how they move in relation to everything around them.

When the Picture Is Mixed

Keep in mind that these weekly and daily charts are suited for the most part for swing trading. You must monitor them, however, and honor any directional bias they indicate. Remember, swing trading is the act of taking countermoves against any existing trend. The bigger picture here identifies which way a current day's trend is likely to go. Taking swing trades in harmony with this direction helps keep your winning percentage high. Buy dips during an uptrend and sell the rallies during downtrends.

But what about the numerous times between trend moves? What happens when weekly charts are headed one direction, while daily charts go another? When both longer-term timeframes move in harmony with each other, you can expect the strongest directional plays to emerge. This synchronized action indicates that the trend move is strong, and making trades in that direction has a high probability of success. When weekly and daily charts diverge, you would still want to take swing trade entries in harmony with the daily chart direction because it usually predicts where the market is headed right now. However, since this move is counter to the weekly chart direction, that usually means it does not have nearly as strong an underlying bias. Therefore, you'd adjust your entry/exit plans accordingly.

PICK YOUR TIME LENGTH TO TRADE

Starting in the volatile markets of the late 1990s, swing trading became known as a one- to three-day trading method. It was not uncommon for massive gains to accrue within hours (or minutes) of a single day. Even in that type of market environment, there were many stocks and other instruments that moved slowly and methodically. Low beta stocks, index and sector shares, and many futures contracts do not whip around in a volatile fashion. Many just plod along rather methodically when following the trend and also while moving against it.

With that in mind, you can eliminate the notion of how long a swing trade should last, and concentrate on what a swing trade is: That is looking for opportunities when the market moves opposite the prevailing trend. Focus on making entries at the point that a countertrend move appears to end and reverses back towards the mean.

While this chapter covered mostly short-term swing trading, the same techniques can be applied to weekly charts to find a trend with daily charts used to time the entry. These trades could be expected to last at least several days and quite possibly a few weeks if the trend is prolonged and stop-loss orders are given enough space or "breathing room" to accommodate volatility or "counter-trend noise."

Even if a trader's intent is to trade low-beta markets over a longer period of time, the very best entries will be found using shorter-term charts than a daily timeframe. Crisp, precise entries are found using intra-day charts, allowing for tighter stops and better risk/reward parameters. That is truly the secret to long-term fiscal success in trading: Proper risk management of a trading account is much more important than simply choosing viable entry points.

No matter what the future holds for the market, whether the indices skyrocket or chug along in a sideways pattern, it is essential to know precisely where you want to buy, sell or hedge. These are the vital steps to creating your financial future — and swing trading can play an important role in getting you there.

PART 5

LOOKING BACK AT LARRY WILLIAMS' LEGENDARY PERFORMANCE

In the world of trading, I don't know if there will ever be another Larry Williams. His performance in the 1987 *World Cup Championship of Futures Trading* has become legendary — an **11,376% return** on his trading account. As with every superstar or titleholder, Larry has become the one to beat. So far, no one has been able to accomplish that. Perhaps one day someone will.

But his numbers alone don't make Larry unique. As someone who knows Larry well — and who was in constant contact with him during his World Cup heyday — I can tell you what makes Larry a true legend: his dedication and his drive to test himself, *even* in the face of tough odds, a deep drawdown or harsh critics.

When Larry entered the competition, he was already an accomplished trader. He had already written several well-received books on futures and stock trading, and he was a popular speaker on the seminar circuit. The *World Cup Championship,* however, provided him with a very public arena in which to test his trading prowess. What happened next is history: He funded his competition account with the minimum requirement of $10,000 on December 15, 1986, and began trading in early January from his office in Solana, Calif. On December 31, 1987, his account balance had ballooned to $1,114,607.

These few statistics hardly tell the story, nor do they explain what makes Larry unique among traders. Along the way, Larry had taken his account to a staggering $2.1 million dollars. Anyone else would have stopped trading. That's what I advised Larry to do. Actually, I thought he was crazy for *not* stopping. But in his mind, traders trade.

So Larry kept trading, only to have his account plummet by $1.4 million to below the $1 million mark. Very few traders could ever recover from that kind of loss — both financially and emotionally. But not Larry. He kept on trading, and ended the year with his unbelievable result.

Trading big sets you up to be a target. Unfortunately, here Larry was no exception. Rumors abounded and critics tried to undermine his performance. He stood up to the scrutiny and to the test of time. In the end, pure trading talent, discipline and a wild trading ride won out.

I'm honored that in these pages, for the first time, Larry has agreed to discuss the peaks and valleys of his historic accomplishment and the toll it exacted on his emotions and personal life. In a lively and candid interview with Chuck Frank, a CBOT T-bond broker from 1981 to 2000 and Managing Director of WorldCupAdvisor.com, Larry discusses the wins, the losses, the critics, and the importance of always trading.

CHAPTER 9

HUGE WINS, MONUMENTAL LOSSES, ANSWERING THE CRITICS, AND ALWAYS TRADING — A CONVERSATION WITH LARRY WILLIAMS

INTERVIEW BY CHUCK FRANK

CF: Larry, by 1987 you were already one of the best-known futures traders in the United States. What motivated you to put your reputation on the line by entering the *World Cup Championship of Futures Trading?*

LW: **I actually didn't think I had a good enough reputation. I thought people perceived me as somebody who just did seminars and wrote books. The rumors are always that guys like that are not for real, they can't trade, they just write books. And so I thought maybe I could show people that I can trade a little bit.**

Before entering the competition, did you consider yourself to be a top futures trader?

Yeah, but I can have a large ego. You know, you always think you're good. You have to have an ego to trade, especially to trade in size. You have to be cautious, but you can't be timid. People who are really timid are never going to start trading 20, 30, 40 contracts. I think you have to be a legend in your own mind to be a big-time trader. You have to really believe in yourself. Is that egotistical or confidence? I don't know what it is, but you have to have it, I know that.

You must have had a target in mind when you entered the competition. Can you put a number on it?

In my mind, I was thinking if you could take $10,000 to $80,000–$100,000, that would be pretty phenomenal. I had taken a couple of $30,000 accounts to a quarter-million dollars, but it was over a longer time period, so I knew what maybe could be done. But trading championships are tough. If you're not correct right away, you're out right away. And the other thing is the vagaries of the marketplace. Some years you see different results in trading championships than other years, and it isn't the traders. It's the markets. Some years the markets present a lot of opportunities and some years they don't. And that's all there is to it.

Was there flexibility in the system you were using during '87?

There's always flexibility in most trading systems. I had just discovered, maybe two years earlier, something now known as volatility breakouts. And I was using volatility breakouts primarily in the S&Ps and the bond market. We knew that if the market moved off some price point — opening, close, average, midpoint, high, whatever — that the move usually continued. We came up with the overall numbers to use, based on what percentage of volatility the range would be and criteria like that, and we programmed it on our own software to see if it worked. We found it was working pretty well.

How was the system run?

We did it by hand. It was rudimentary. TradeStation didn't exist; there wasn't anything as nice and as simple as what we now have.

On January 6, 1987 you closed out a small loser on a one-lot T-bond trade. After 10 trades you were still in the red by a few hundred dollars. Not exactly an auspicious start. Did those first few trades concern you?

You always pay attention to every trade. But my entire trading life I haven't been concerned about my past trades, because past trades do not predict the future. There's a great example of it, in fact, because if you would look at the first trades you'd say, "Oh, this guy is going to blow up; he won't set world records that won't be beaten." So the past doesn't predict much of anything. You can't say "Oh, my gosh, I had a losing trade!" Of course, you prefer not to have losers. Did I want my first trade to be a winning trade? Yeah, I did. I didn't get it, but I was still in the game. Because I was using a money-management formula, I knew I wouldn't get blown away too much. I knew I was going to be in the game for a while, even in a worst-case scenario.

In retrospect, what's really interesting is to go on the Internet today and find people who say that the contest was rigged, that I had one account I put the winning trades in and one I put the losing trades in.* Well, here's proof positive. Why would I want to have losing trades to start the championship with? Early on is exactly when you've got to have the most money. You've got to get a jump on everybody in a trading competition, but like I said you can't look back. You can study from your errors, but you can't have your errors become your focal point because otherwise you'll choke.

*[*These rampant rumors precipitated a Commodity Futures Trading Commission (CFTC) audit in 1988, which identified no improprieties.]*

You then hit a streak that may well have been the turning point of your year. You reeled off eight consecutive winners, trading no more than a six-lot of T-bonds or S&Ps, to move your account ahead by more than $23,000 and give yourself some breathing room. Had that early streak gone the other way, your year might have been over.

Sure, it's always true, what if I had a bunch of losing trades? But a trader's supposed to have more winning trades than losing trades. So every streak is the combination of what the market presents and what the trader can do with it.

Once a trade was entered and your stop was in place, would you hang around the office all day monitoring every tick of the market?

Yeah, back then I was usually watching the market all the time, it was right in front of me. I was there for almost every tick.

Was there any intra-day activity that could occur to prompt you to override the system once a trade was initiated and exit prematurely?

I don't know that I did. The system trades were mechanical — here's a buy order, here's the stop, here's where to get out — but there were also things that would happen with intra-day market indicators along the way that would give me buys and sells, and I had to be there to watch that. I was looking for certain indicators to take place so that I could do certain things; that's why I was looking at the screens all day.

Did you make any impulse trades that were not indicated by the system or by intra-day indicators?

I'm certain I did, I mean we all do. I would lie if I said I didn't do some on impulse.

In early March came an incredible stretch of 19 winners in 21 trades, during which your account value appreciated by more than $100,000. You had moved your size up to 20 and 30 lots. Can you explain the money-management technique you employed?

I was using something called the Kelly formula that Ralph Vince had popularized. I found the Kelly formula in a little blackjack book, and Ralph and I started fooling around with it and it led to the whole thing of money management. Actually J.L. Kelly Jr. originally devised the formula for the flow of electrons through circuitry. But he said you could apply it to blackjack betting to measure risk/rewards, too, and then we applied it to trading. It's very wild and it will exponentially increase the number of contracts you're trading when you're winning, so you see that we stepped up from 1 lot to 30 lots rapidly. But when you lose money you've got to step back down. I use a variation of that in my own trading today.

Can you explain the specific formula?

Let's put F as amount of capital to trade. The amount of capital equals the payoff ratio — that's the risk/reward ratio — plus 1, divided by probability — the system accuracy — minus 1.

$$F = (\text{payoff ratio} + 1) \div (\text{probability} - 1)$$

I did some tables on it. Let's say your system is 40% correct and has a 2.5 risk/reward ratio, you'll use 16% of your money. If your system is 63% correct with a 2.5 risk reward/ratio, you'll use 55% of your money on every trade. So it varies by accuracy. It's a matrix of the accuracy versus a risk/reward ratio.

Towards the end of March '87, you took a hit of nearly $43,000 on a 50-lot bond trade. But you came right back and made $220,000 on your next seven trades. Is it hard to get back on the horse after a loss of that magnitude?

I considered it sort of a dent. At that point, you're kind of a little goofy in your head because you've seen these huge equity increases. And suddenly I realized I was doing something that hadn't happened before. This is a bad analogy, but in a very small way I can understand what Barry Bonds and Mark McGuire have gone through. I know it's totally different, and they're so much greater in what they've done than I'll ever be, but I can relate to the sense that, "Hey you're doing something that's historic." And there's a lot of excitement and pride in saying, "Yeah, something's going on here that I'm almost not in control of myself."

I really felt that way a lot. It's almost like I could walk on the waters of the commodity markets because I was so in sync with them. You're just in that zone. And then what catches up to you is that your apparent success brings out a lot of critics. A lot of people are looking over your shoulder, and that's pressure. I've always had that because I've been in the public eye. I had always had it before, but *never* to that extent.

How did you know that people were watching what you were doing?

People from the floor would call when they saw I was suddenly trading large lots in what had been a small account. People had found out what was going on. The rumor got around and there were some people who said that it was rigged, and some people who said I wasn't any good because I was just trading bonds and S&Ps. So you'll see times that year where I traded (soy)beans and (pork)bellies and stuff, just to say "Hey look, I am good; I can trade what I want to. And darn it all, I'm gonna do it." And so some trades in there were simply to respond to critics. It had nothing to do with really making money. It was to say, "Look, you give me a market and if I'm focused I can trade that sucker." And so some of those trades were really for that purpose only.

And then suddenly I thought, "Well, this is crazy, I'm trading to win a championship and create history, not to reply to my critics." But you get caught up in the reply to your critics. And they're everywhere, and I deserved a lot of it, too. I brought it on myself.

Why do you say that?

Well, I don't know that I have an obnoxious personality, but maybe it's a flamboyant personality when it comes to trading in the markets. And I've always tried to separate myself from the crowd a little bit. When you do good research and good writing and good presentations, it draws out critics. Swashbucklers have people who want to swashbuckle against them.

After closing out a 105-lot winner of $192,000 on April 29, your account balance was a whopping $872,000. You had made two-thirds of a million dollars in 20 trading days and had a lock on first place in the World Cup competition. Were there any thoughts about cashing in your chips at that point?

Yeah, there were several points along the way early in the year where you're saying, "Well, you know, I've done it." But we had a lot of time left, and it would have felt pretty hollow to say, "Well, all I really did was get a jump on other people here, then I took my marbles and went home." I don't think real men do that.

Was there anybody who was giving you any kind of run for your money that year?

Oh yes, there were. There were a bunch of us in the pack at the $40,000 to $50,000 level. There was pressure. I was worried about where I was: second, third, fourth, second, third, first, second. It was up and down there for a while.

By the end of May, your account balance had been more than chopped in half. You had stepped up your size and 100-lots were common in both the bonds and the S&Ps, but the magic seemed to have worn off. How were you sleeping?

Same as always. This is what I've done all my life. Some people look at this kind of trading and they go, "Oh my gosh." Well, I have that same awe for a mechanic, because I don't know how to fix mechanical things. When somebody brings in a junk heap I say, "No way the guy can do this," and he repairs it. But that's what he should do because that's what his career is and he lives with that.

And that's what I've done throughout my career, so it's no great skill or anything of great awe. It's just what I've done all my life. I've had ups and downs of huge magnitude in my trading and so it's nothing new. It's the life of a trader.

In June, you started the long climb back. You made 38 round turns that month, averaging 50 lots per trade, and clawed your way back to nearly $780,000 by the end of the month. The trades you mentioned in other products — Euros, T-bills, gold, silver, cattle, pork bellies, and later Swiss Francs and coffee — were starting to appear. In addition to making the statement that "I can trade any market," did you see some good opportunities in those other markets?

Responding to critics was the main reason to be in the other markets. All these rumors were going around saying I can do this and not that. Gosh, that was 15 years ago, and I'm certain I was pretty cocky, maybe even an obnoxious person, because success kind of makes you that way. You know, suddenly you're doing things that haven't happened before.

Although the trades you made in other markets were on balance marginally profitable, they sidetracked you from focusing your full attention on your main trading targets of bonds and S&Ps. Do you regret making those trades?

Oh, I can't regret the past. If you're in this business of speculating, you never regret the past. The past can't have you. I don't look at the past; I don't care about it. The past is over, it's dead, it's history.

A losing trade of $360,000 on a huge 237-lot in the bonds late in July wiped out most of your profit for the month. Three more losing trades followed quickly, and you had lost close to half a million dollars in one week. How were your nerves holding up?

It didn't feel real good. I thought maybe I had lost the touch.

Were you thinking that maybe you never had it?

No, I don't think that as much as I was thinking, "I've been through this before." You know, I'd seen other swings like that

before. I'd said to myself, "This kind of thing happens. I screwed some things up here. Can you get back on track, Williams? You gotta get back in that groove. Wherever that flow is, you gotta get back in it."

When you hit the skids with a system you've developed, do you wind up saying, "The system lost money today" or do you say, "I screwed up and lost money today?"

Both can happen. You can screw up and lose money because you don't follow the system or the system can lose money. You're not immune from either. Even if you're following the system and you're not screwing up personally, it's always going to be an up and down business. If you're looking for perfection and money every day, you're in the wrong business. That's not what this is about.

In the extreme volatility of August '87, you reverted to your original MO, limiting your trades to the bond and S&P pits. On the strength of winners of $130,000, $200,000, $114,000, and $208,000 — all in the bonds — you finished the month with more than a million dollars in your account. You had overcome the big setback and were finally above the seven-figure mark. Why not stop and leave well enough alone?

Greed is a disease of the Western world. Plus, again, I was in a trading championship and I wanted to still push the pedal to the metal. The point wasn't to get to August or October; the point was to get to the end of the year. And how would it have looked if I took my marbles and walked away early, especially at that point with all of the background noise around Larry Williams? In a way, I cannot express to you what it was like. People would call me and tell me about the rumors and complain about things to me. There was a lot of attention to it. I figured in my mind that I was going to go to the end of this thing. I was not going to walk away because that would be one more thing for the critics to harangue at — "Oh well, he quit early."

And I also didn't know in my mind how far I could take it, where I could take it, what I could do with it. The hell with all the critics and stuff, what could Larry Williams do? I knew I had my act

together and things were going well. What could I do? I wanted to know that.

With 100- and 200-lot trades common in your account, the quality of fills in wild markets must have been a huge issue for you. Were you satisfied with the bond and S&P pit brokers who were selected to fill for traders in the competition?

Well, yes. I was also managing accounts at that time for Robbins (Trading Company) as well as another firm. Joel (Robbins) had picked some people that he thought were pretty good on the floor filling orders, especially in size. I'd gone to Chicago, met with the brokers, talked with them. I felt I had good people assisting me to fill orders.

Amid tremendous volatility, you stepped up your size with bond trades in excess of 400 contracts in September. Your $10,000 stake had swelled to $2,042,967. Any thought at that juncture of putting the flag on top of Everest and saying "Here it is?"

No.

Was there any threshold you could have crossed that would have prompted you to stop trading? Three million? Five million?

No, there was no number, no dollar amount at that point. The goal was get to the end of the contest and let's see where you are, Larry, while exposing yourself to a lot of risk along the way. It was a yearlong trading championship and real people stay for the full ride.

And to this day, this is the first time that I've ever referenced those trades of '87, the first time I ever really talked about it. I decided when I was through that I didn't want to look at it, and I haven't looked at it since. To me it was like, "Hey, you know, I did it. I'm through with that; go on to another thing in my life." I guess I'm not big on looking back.

Did you have a thought as to the maximum quantities you could trade without disturbing the market?

I felt I could trade up to 300 S&Ps, and I could probably trade 5,000 bonds at that point without disturbing the market. But that doesn't mean I was right. (Laughs)

In the plunge of October '87 you got hammered. Two trades alone cost $800,000. The $2 million milestone was in the rear-view mirror. What was your frame of mind then?

During the big equity drawdown, I was actually in Africa on a safari. The trading was left to a couple of guys in my office because it was automatic. And we unfortunately sold bonds, and in the flight to quality of the crash of '87 bonds gapped up. I didn't have a clue what was going on at the time, and by the time they got out we had a bit of an equity dip there that you alluded to.

Were you literally on safari?

Yeah, I was in Kenya. We were on our way to the Mt. Kenya Safari Club and the little guy who came to pick us up with this two-seater plane said, "Oh the stock market's crashed, the stock market's crashed." I said, "Yeah, I know, it was going down when I left." And he said, "Oh, no, it's down big time now." When we got to the safari club I could hear people say, "It's down 200 points" — and 200 points back then was down a lot. Then they said, "It's down 300," and then, "No it's down 500." Finally I heard somebody say, "It's down 600." And at that point about half the room got up and made phone calls to America to see what had gone on. When I found out what went on, I said, "Oh, I wonder what those guys did? Are we right or are we wrong?" We could have been right, too, you know. But we were wrong.

You didn't check to see what your positions were?

No, I did not know. I thought, "Well, I know the market was down 600 points. Now I've got an option here. I could find out if I'm losing or winning or I could enjoy the safari. If I'm winning I'm going to be really wrapped up and I won't enjoy this, and if I'm losing for sure I won't enjoy this, so you know what? I'm not going to find out." So I didn't have a clue what was going on. Intuitively, I didn't think it was good, and maybe that's why I didn't call. But I continued on the safari, and two days later I got hit with malaria and that was pretty severe. Getting malaria was a lot worse than the equity dip we had. My mind really wasn't too concerned about trading at that point. It was just like, "I gotta get over this to get outta here and then come back to America." I had no strength at all for the first four or five days.

Did you ever total up your losses on Black Monday that October?

Oh, I don't know, you'd have to look at it. Again, you know I don't look back. I really like what Satchel Paige said: "Don't look back. Something might be gaining on you." I never really looked at the numbers, but I know it was like a million bucks or something. Somebody pointed it out to me.

Did the pressure of these huge swings spill over into your personal life at all?

Sure. Because I had way too much money on every single trade, I think that my emotions were affected and that I probably wasn't a particularly pleasant person to live with. I'm not manic-depressive, but it does take you in that direction when you make a quarter million bucks one day and then lose a quarter million the next. My emotions fluctuated and I tried to control them so it didn't wash over into my personal life, but it did. I think my family pretty much understood what was going on.

Even after that debacle, which included a $638,000 loser on a 400-lot in the bonds, you never missed a beat. Your account continued trading while you were recuperating in Kenya, and you picked up the order-entry yourself when you got back home. You traded to the wire — December 28th, 29th, 30th, and 31st.

Yeah, I felt that I had an obligation to do that. Some people in trading championships get up to some point and quit, and they may win the championship or somebody may sneak up on them. Obviously, nobody was going to sneak up on me at that point. But I still felt there was an obligation to continue doing what I had done — and that was to trade — and short of that was pulling up short and not walking the walk of a real trader.

When you closed out the last trade of the year on December 31 and posted the final account balance of $1,114,607, were you feeling more satisfaction or relief?

That's a really great question. It was relief that it was over. I had been under this microscope from everybody within the business and it was nice to suddenly be out of the limelight and off stage. It was really nice.

You have not traded in the World Cup since the historic '87 performance. But you did commemorate the 10th anniversary of the victory in a dramatic way. Can you talk about that?

Well, yeah, again maybe one of my weaknesses is that I respond to critics too much. But the rumors were still out that I had rigged the trading championship with Robbins Trading Company, which makes little sense because there's a winner every year. They don't have to create a winner; there's always a winner. But myopic people don't understand that, and that was bothering me. And then some people said, "Oh, he's a has-been, he's washed up," and so I thought, "Well, let's do something on the 10th anniversary; I'm going to teach one of my kids to trade." And so I taught one of my daughters (actress Michelle Williams) a little bit about trading and I said, "Hey, if you've got the money, why don't you see what you can do?" And she said, "OK, let's do it, Dad."

Was the $10,000 stake her money and her risk?

Yeah, she had done so many TV shows and movies and she was making pretty good money for a 16-year-old kid. Actually, she was making pretty good money for an adult. The interesting thing about Michelle was that when she won, a lot of people said, "This is bogus, her dad was doing the trades," or "How can she trade; she's a 16-year-old kid? Kids can't open up commodity accounts!" People were wrong on both counts.

Michelle had become legally emancipated to sign a contract for Warner Brothers for one of the movies she did, and so she had legal right to contract. She was entering the orders herself, but then after three or four months in the competition, "Dawson's Creek" (the TV

series) began, and she was getting cast calls at weird hours like three o'clock in the morning. She said, "Dad, I just can't do all this." And I said, "Well, you know what, just call Gene (Payne) at Robbins and tell him to follow the hotline." So she called Gene and told him to just follow the hotline with this money management thing we had talked about, which was one contract for every $10,000.

Michelle ran away with the '97 title with an even 1,000% return, adding $100,094 to her bank account. Any other family members we should know about?

You know, they don't want to trade. Nobody's really interested. Even the actress-daughter doesn't trade anymore.

Under what circumstances would you consider participating in the *World Cup Championship of Futures Trading* again?

I'm thinking of doing it again soon. There will be rumors again on the next big anniversary (the 20th in 2007), but I don't know if I can wait that long. But it's hard to do all the lecturing and teaching I do and still trade that aggressively. You have to really be focused to do this. I'd like to do something that's really flamboyant, at least every 10 years, to show that I'm still around. Maybe I'm just looking for an excuse here. We'll see what happens.

Would you start with the minimum of $15,000?

Yeah, start small. That's the trouble. A lot of people figure there's the old adage in Las Vegas: To win big you gotta bet big. Totally wrong. You know how the house takes your money. You want to start small with $15,000. You can take that someplace, and what can you lose — $15,000 at the worst? Can you make that back? Sure, in a heartbeat. But if you start with $150,000 or $200,000 and dump that, that's hard money to get back.

Is there anything that people can learn from '87 in terms of systems trading and living through drawdowns?

Yeah, they can learn a couple of things. They can draw from the fact that when I went through down periods, I didn't walk away; I didn't let the event get to me, I continued doing what I was doing. I was way over-leveraged and they should learn to do less than what I did. They should also realize that somebody can show you a track record — hypothetical or real-time trading — and the human mind just buzzes through it but doesn't understand the emotions of living through two or three losing trades. The fact that my name is on it or a system has appeared to work in the past, guarantees nothing. The fingerprints of the past are never seen in the future.

If you compete again, what would the primary motivation be?

To win. To compete and to shut people up. It'll show that I'm still around and I can still trade. The critics and the naysayers out there are not just critics of me, they're critics of this industry, they say everybody loses trading commodities. Well, I've shown on a somewhat consistent basis that that's fallacious. And you know I don't mind showing that and doing it again. And so, I need to find some interesting way of doing it.

Do you feel in your heart that you can replicate what you did in '87?

No, because that was a combination of a very low margin and a very wild market. If those conditions come again, even then I don't know if I'm going to be skilled enough to do it. Maybe I am washed up. You know, that's always in the back of my mind. At 60 years of age you say, "Hey, it could be my better days are behind me," and so you have to wonder about that. But you have to have the right conditions. Can I go in and win a contest? Not at will, but you know, I can compete, I can get in there. I might be first or second or third, but I'd like to think I'd be in the top bracket. Win? Maybe, maybe not. But will I show that I can do it? Yeah. And that's the goal really, to show that it can still be done.

I would really like to encourage people to look at the championships, all of them, Robbins' as well as the others. See what type of strategies win these trading championships, so you know where to invest your time and your own research and education. That's critical. We can learn so much from the styles that win these championships. Because there're a lot of methodologies out there that purport to make money, so let's look at which ones win the trading championships to see which are the most effective.

In your opinion, will someone surpass your 11,376% performance in the next 20 years?

I hope so. I don't see why not. We know more about the markets now than we did then, and we understand things with more knowledge, so hopefully somebody can beat the pants off me.

Do you think that a top finish in the *World Cup Championship,* in and of itself, qualifies an individual to give advice to other traders?

I think it needs to be respected. Any of these guys who have a top finish did something that no one else did that year. In this business, you learn to respect success.

Is there any futures trading championship in your mind that's comparable in prestige and magnitude to the World Cup?

No, the *Robbins World Cup Trading Championship* has the track record. It's created some great traders and a lot of careers. I think that if a guy or gal thinks that they're good, they ought to hop on this thing to test themselves. It will bring out things in you; it will make you greater than you are. I know the *Robbins World Cup Trading Championship* made Larry Williams a different person. And I'm certain that it's done that for all of the winners. Not only getting to know Joel and the people at Robbins, but in terms of your own sense of yourself. You don't have to win; I think just being in it will change your ability to trade.

What did it specifically tell you about yourself?

That money management is so critical. That I was still very inadequate in a lot of things.

You have a million reasons to feel quite adequate about 1987.

There you go.

WORLD CUP CHAMPIONSHIP OF FUTURES TRADING® HIGHLIGHTS

Robert Bloch: 1999 winner (non-professional division) with a 179% return; 1999 runner-up (professional division) with a 216% return. Winner of a record six trophies overall.

David Cash: 2001 winner with a 53% return.

John Holsinger: 2002 winner and runner-up with returns of 608% and 304%, respectively.

Chuck Hughes: 1999 winner (professional division) with a 315% return. Winner of five trophies overall.

John Mills: 1989 winner (non-professional division) with a 53% return. Winner of four trophies overall.

Austin Passamonte: Austin Passamonte is a non-competitive-status member of the WorldCupAdvisor.com staff.

Neil Peplinski: 1998 winner (non-professional division) with a 94% return.

Kurt Sakaeda: 2000 winner with a 595% return. Winner of two trophies overall.

Larry Williams: 1987 winner with a record 11,376% return.

The World Cup Championship of Futures Trading® is sponsored by Robbins Trading Company.

WHO ARE THE WORLD CUP ADVISORS?

Robert Bloch's accomplishments in the *World Cup Championship of Futures Trading*® are unparalleled. Highlights include a 1999 victory in the non-professional division with a 179% return *and* a second-place finish in the professional division with a 216% return the same year. He placed at least two accounts in the World Cup top-10 four out of five years from 1998 to 2002, and has received a record six Bull & Bear trophies for top-three finishes. Mr. Bloch is a Commodity Trading Advisor and manages a $50 million bond portfolio for a bank in California, where he lives.

In 2001, **David Cash** joined an elite group of traders who have won the *World Cup Championship of Futures Trading*® title in their first attempt. Although Cash's winning performance was a historically low 53%, he captured the title during a notoriously difficult trading year in which he more than doubled the account appreciation of the second-place finisher. Mr. Cash is an engineer who, prior to actively trading the markets, served a stint at NASA's Johnson Space Center working on the space station project in 1994 and 1995. He lives in Austin, TX.

John Holsinger accomplished an unprecedented "double" in the 2002 *World Cup Championship of Futures Trading*® by capturing the title with a whopping 608% return, *and* nailing down second place with a healthy 304% in a partnership account with system designer and friend Mike Dietch. Mr. Holsinger is a Commodity Trading Advisor and is president and principal trader of Potomac Advisors, Inc. of Alexandria, VA. He is also a Certified Public Accountant.

Chuck Hughes won the 1999 *World Cup Championship of Futures Trading*® in a hotly contested year that saw three accounts appreciate more than 100%. His 315% return captured the overall title that year; he has earned a total of five trophies since first competing in the World Cup Trading Championships in 1994. Mr. Hughes is a Commodity Trading Advisor and a retired airline pilot. He is the author of several home study trading courses and lives in New Jersey.

John Mills is a four-time trophy winner in *World Cup Championship of Futures Trading*® competition, including a first-place finish in the non-professional division in 1989. Mr. Mills is a Commodity Trading Advisor who trades a wide variety of futures products as well as the Forex market. He lives in Ohio.

Austin Passamonte brings a wealth of securities, futures and options trading expertise to subscribers on both the WorldCupAdvisor.com and CoiledMarkets.com web sites on a daily basis. Mr. Passamonte is an active trader and a Commodity Trading Advisor. He lives in New York.

Neil Peplinski leaped to the front of the competitive trading crowd in 1998 by scoring a *World Cup Championship of Futures Trading*® victory in his first appearance, producing a 95% return in the non-professional division. His performance came within a whisker (4.35%) of topping all competitiors that year. Mr. Peplinski is a Commodity Trading Advisor and lives in the Chicago area.

Kurt Sakaeda's winning return of 595% in the 2000 *World Cup Championship of Futures Trading*® left his competitors in the dust, as second place checked in at 138%. With his unique seasonal trading method, he came back in 2001 with another strong showing, placing seventh at 63%. Mr. Sakaeda is a Commodity Trading Advisor who lives in Chicago. He has won two World Cup trophies.

Larry Williams' brought a flood of attention to the *World Cup Championship of Futures Trading*® in 1987, when he ran a $10,000 account to $1,114,607 during a volatile year of trading. His 11,376% return stands as the top performance in World Cup history and marks Mr. Williams' only appearance in the futures trading competition. Larry Williams resides in California.

ABOUT THE EDITORS

Chuck Frank

Chuck Frank's career combines experience as both a writer and trader. He spent seven years as a sportswriter with The Chicago Tribune's Suburban Trib supplement before moving to the 30-year T-bond pit at the Chicago Board of Trade, where he worked as an independent broker and trader for 19 years. He left the trading floor to develop the WorldCupAdvisor.com Web site in 2000. Frank's first non-fiction book was published in 1980.

Patricia Crisafulli

Patricia Crisafulli is a former business journalist working for a number of leading news organizations including Reuters America, where she was a correspondent on the equities desk in the Chicago bureau. She is now a writer in the Chicago area and has ghost-written several books on business and investing. She is also the author of her own non-fiction book.

RECOMMENDED READING

The Investor's Quotient: The Psychology of Successful Investing in Commodities & Stocks, 2nd Edition

By Jake Bernstein

"The Investor's Quotient" offers a complete and highly effective investment psychology regimen that puts traders on the road to consistent profits. Discover practical, proven techniques for sharpening perception, developing positive attitude and confidence, learning from failures, losing less on bad trades, making more on profitable ones, and more.

$18.95 Item# BC70x-11481

Portfolio Management Formulas: Mathematical Trading Methods for the Futures, Options, and Stock Markets

By Ralph Vince

"Belongs on the shelf of every informed investor." — Tom DeMark. Optimize your trading system by exploiting the rules of probability and the principles of modern portfolio management.

$90.00 Item# BC70x-2821

Stock Trader's Almanac 2005

By Jeffrey Hirsch

"The Stock Trader's Almanac" is a practical investment tool with a wealth of information organized in a calendar format. It encapsulates all the historical price information on the stock market, provides monthly and daily reminders, and alerts users to seasonal opportunities and dangers. The data in the Almanac is some of the cleanest in the business, and the analysis used by savvy professionals from well-known money managers to journalists.

$22.95 Item# BC70x-1796295

Cartoon Guide to Statistics

By Larry Gonick and Woolcott Smith

The "Cartoon Guide to Statistics" covers all the central ideas of modern statistics: the summary and display of data, probability in gambling and medicine, random variables, Bernoulli Trails, the Central Limit Theorem, hypothesis testing, confidence interval estimation, and much more — all explained in simple, clear, and funny illustrations.

$16.95 Item# BC70x-496860

Geometry of Markets

By Bryce Gilmore

"Geometry of Markets" will give you an insight into the natural order at work in all free trading markets. This information would normally be unavailable for such a reasonable price. Market analysis is reduced to a science by applying graphic representation of the geometry relating price movement in time.

$89.00 Item# BC70x-11390

Zurich Axioms

By Max Gunther

Designed to lessen risk while increasing rewards, this investment guide outlines the strategies that made the Swiss bankers and businessmen wealthy beyond belief. Gunther provides 12 major Axioms that can help anyone succeed in investing — Swiss style.

$18.95 Item# BC70x-1513149

Market Wizards: Interviews with Top Traders

By Jack Schwager

How do the world's top traders amass millions? This classic bestseller takes you into the minds of the greatest traders Wall Street has ever known. In depth interviews with key players expose every facet of their strategies.

$17.00 Item# BC70x-2243

The New Market Wizards: Conversations with America's Top Traders

By Jack Schwager

In the classic hard cover version, this title is a true investment "Bible." In depth interviews with key players expose every facet of their winning strategies for consistently outperforming peers. See how you can do it, too!

$39.95 Item# BC70x-2106

Stock Market Wizards: Interviews with America's Top Stock Traders

By Jack Schwager

Now in paperback, "Stock Market Wizards" by Trader's Hall of Fame Award winner Jack Schwager. Revised and updated, the paperback edition of the hardcover best-seller contains follow-up interviews with some of the "wizards" from the original edition as well as an additional chapter about a new "Stock Market Wizard."

$15.95 Item# BC70x-959606

WorldCupAdvisor.com

Live Update Service

John Holsinger (Holsinger E-mini Russell) - Copyright© WorldCupAdvisor.com Ltd. 2001 - Microsoft Internet ...

Orders | **Open Positions** | **Closed Positions** | **Comments**

Order# Status	Date/Time Placed	Replaces Replaced by	Cancels Cancelled by	Action/Qty Symbol/Exp.	Type Time Frame	Price	Fill Price	Date/Time Filled	Strike Price	Put Call	Open Close	Stop Limit Price	Spread Price
50112 Filled	8/27/04 10:30:31	50081		Sell 1 ER 09/04	Stop Day	54900	54900	08/27/04 10:53:25					
50082 Replaced	8/27/04 09:30:41	50113		Sell 1 ER 09/04	Stop Day	54520							
50081 Replaced	8/27/04 09:30:33	50112		Sell 1 ER 09/04	Stop Day	54520							
50031 Replaced	8/27/04 08:49:05	50081		Sell 1 ER 09/04	Stop Day	54500							
50030 Cancelled	8/27/04 08:48:44		50121	Sell 1 ER 09/04	MIT Day	55710							
50023 Replaced	8/27/04 08:33:19	50082		Sell 1 ER 09/04	Stop Day	54500							
50022 Filled	8/27/04 08:33:01			Buy 1 ER 09/04	Stop Day	54810	54830	08/27/04 08:48:00					
40341 Filled	8/26/04 15:13:06			Buy 1 ER 09/04	Mkt Day		54540	08/26/04 15:13:05					
40338 Cancels	8/26/04 15:11:19		40274	Buy 1 ER 09/04	Stop Day	54840							
40335 Cancels	8/26/04 15:07:20		40124	Buy 1 ER 09/04	MIT Day	53940							

What is the premise of the WorldCupAdvisor.com site?

WorldCupAdvisor.com is the live trading home for nationally recognized futures, forex and stock traders. We broadcast their trading in real time so that our subscribers can attempt to make the very same trades. Some of our "Live Update" accounts are entered in the World Cup Trading Championships®; all are trading real money in real time.

What do I get for my Live Update subscription dollars?

You get access to a real-time visual display of the Live Update account(s) to which you are subscribed. We maintain separate screens for orders entered (below), open positions, closed positions (above), and commentary. Advisors utilize the commentary screen to clarify trade activity and provide instructions.

How do I duplicate the trading taking place in a Live Update account?

Some subscribers place orders themselves in online accounts or call their broker with instructions. Many elect to sign a Letter of Direction and have Robbins Trading Company follow the signals on their behalf through Robbins' System Assist® AutoTrade™ service. Subscriptions to some accounts are available only to AutoTrade™ clients.

Profit or loss shown below is based on actual entry and exit prices, but does not include commissions or exchange fees.

Orders | **Open Positions** | **Closed Positions** | **Comments**

	Symbol	Expiration	Buy Qty	Sell Qty	Buy Price	Sell Price	P/S
8/27/2004 8:48:00 AM	ER	09/04	1		54830		
8/27/2004 10:53:24 AM	ER	09/04		1		54900	+70.00
8/26/2004 3:13:05 PM	ER	09/04	1		54540		
8/26/2004 9:30:22 AM	ER	09/04		1		54840	+300.00
8/25/2004 8:13:06 PM	ER	09/04	1		54870		
8/25/2004 7:30:52 PM	ER	09/04		1		54920	+50.00
8/25/2004 4:00:45 PM	ER	09/04	1		54390		
8/25/2004 7:30:52 PM	ER	09/04		1		54920	+530.00
8/24/2004 8:07:54 PM	ER	09/04	1		54530		
8/24/2004 3:22:22 PM	ER	09/04		1		54190	-340.00
8/24/2004 1:30:21 PM	ER	09/04	1		54760		
8/24/2004 2:34:08 PM	ER	09/04		1		54400	-360.00
8/23/2004 8:13:32 PM	ER	09/04	1		54400		
8/23/2004 2:30:35 PM	ER	09/04		1		54610	+210.00
8/20/2004 1:34:41 PM	ER	09/04	1		53870		
8/20/2004 7:35:14 PM	ER	09/04		1		54760	+890.00
8/20/2004 1:34:40 PM	ER	09/04	1		53870		

How will I know when there is activity in the account(s) to which I'm subscribed?

When you're logged into a Live Update account, an Instant Message will appear any time there is new activity. If you keep your computer speakers on, a bell will ring to alert you to the incoming message. Just click "close" on the Instant Message to view the new activity. An email notification also accompanies each new activity.

Is there a guarantee that these renowned traders will trade profitably?

Of course not. However, our traders do have a history of success. Many have posted top-3 finishes in the World Cup Trading Championships®.

How do I determine which account is best suited for my trading style?

A button on our homepage links to the complete closed-position history of all of our accounts. Call us and we will be happy to recommend an account that is suitable for you.

Trading futures, stocks and forex involve substantial risk of loss and may not be suitable for everyone. Past performance is not indicative of future results.